GINGER STANDS HER GROUND

VIRGINIA FORD

FIFTH
AVENUE
PRESS

Ginger Stands Her Ground

Copyright © 2017 by Virginia Ford

Editor: Alex Kourvo

Illustration and Layout: Ann Arbor District Library

Fifth Avenue Press is a locally focused and publicly owned publishing imprint of the Ann Arbor District Library. It is dedicated to supporting the local writing community by promoting the production of original fiction, non-fiction and poetry written for children, teens and adults.

Printed in the United States of America

First Printing, 2017

ISBN: 978-1-947989-11-5 (*Hardcover*), 978-1-947989-12-2 (*Paperback*)

Fifth Avenue Press

305 S Fifth Ave

Ann Arbor, MI 48104

fifthavenue.press

In loving memory of my parents,
Arthur John and Virginia Mary Fagan Visel,
who encouraged me to read and to stand my ground

Mom and Dad in October of 1953.

AUTHOR'S NOTE

I have carried this project in my heart since my teen years. Books about living with a disability like polio were—and still are—scarce. I yearned to read something that I could relate to and vowed that someday I would add to the small collection available. Retirement gave me the opportunity and the mature perspective to tell my story before it got lost in the fogginess of time. My intent was to write an informative and inspiring book that would serve as a beacon of hope in meeting the challenges of life. I have tried my best to record the people, places, and events in this memoir as accurately as possible, taking into account my youth and the emotions involved.

THROUGH THE WINDOW

"CATCH ME IF YOU CAN," I teased, pumping my four-year-old legs hard and leading my younger brother in a merry chase around our backyard. Our dog Blackie raced hot on my heels. Making a swift turn in a last-ditch effort to lose Charlie, I ducked under the dry sheets hanging on the clothesline just as he stretched out and tagged me on the shoulder shouting, "You're it!"

Winded, we sprawled on our backs in the sweet-smelling grass, listening to Mom as she sang, "Oh, what a beautiful morning" while unpinning clothes from another line under puffy clouds floating in the bluest sky. A whistle interrupted our rest.

I jumped to my feet and spotted Dad holding a string of bluegill as he made his way home through the field from Wylie Lake. "Fresh fish for dinner tonight!" he exclaimed.

Charlie sprang to life as he broke into a trot. "Come on, Ginger! I'll race you to Dad!"

"You better go faster if you wanna beat me," I laughed. Turning on the speed, my bare feet pounded the ground. We flew to Dad.

"Whoa! Hold on. You two look like yearlings racing head-to-head," Dad said.

I grabbed Dad's tackle box and skipped along beside him as Charlie slipped the string of fish out of his other hand with a grin.

My internal stopwatch always freezes this moment, like an arrested scene in a movie. On this splendid summer day in 1950, I was the happiest barefoot girl on the planet.

If only every day could bring such simple pleasures. But life had other plans. How could I know my legs would soon fail me, leaving me to stumble into the future?

A FEW MONTHS LATER, a moody gray day broke in November. I woke with a raging fever, sore throat, and a stiff neck. With a worried look on his face, Dad carried me downstairs to the couch in our family room near the Kalamazoo stove. Here I spent a miserable day. By nightfall, delirious and shivering with chills, I was brought upstairs to my parents' feather bed. During the night, Mom remained by my side as I repeatedly cried out for sips of water. The next day, nothing changed. After the milkman's weekly delivery, Mom tilted my head so I could drink a glass of chocolate milk. I couldn't keep it down.

Suddenly, I needed help to get to the bathroom. I could hardly raise my head off the pillow, let alone have anyone touch it. Alarmed, my parents called Doc Wylie, who made a house call. My temperature hit 104 degrees, he reported. After examining my ears, eyes, nose, and throat and studying my lethargic limbs, Doc Wylie offered his diagnosis. "This is just a bad cold and the flu." He prescribed bed rest, aspirin, and plenty of liquids, with a mandate to my mother. "Get that fever down!"

Grandma, who lived next door, came over to look at me.

She stood next to the couch waving a dollar bill and promising, "Honey, it's all yours if you raise your leg."

I tried, but I couldn't. A deep sorrow flooded me and I sobbed. A four-year-old knows when a big wave is washing her out to sea.

Shortly afterwards, Dad refused any more delay. "That's it. We need to get her to the hospital!"

In 1950, hospitals were a last and rare resort. Bundling me in a pink blanket, he carried me to the family car and deposited me into Mom's waiting arms. He rushed us to the University of Michigan Hospital emergency entrance, where the medical attendant asked Dad to roll down his car window. They told him my symptoms and Dr. Wylie's diagnosis. Before we even had a chance to get out of the car, he said bluntly, "I'm sorry sir. I don't believe our facility can help your daughter. A contagious disease is on a rampage, and we're taking all precautionary steps." He directed Dad to the isolation building. Patients suspected of being contagious were quarantined in a dinky yellow building that loomed in the shadow of the massive main hospital. In its former life, the structure had served as a laundry. Now it accommodated twenty-four beds reserved for quarantined patients.

Before even getting inside, I became delirious.

Somewhere partway between consciousness and unconsciousness, I woke to blinding overhead lights. Squinting, I saw an old doctor dressed in white and wearing a mask that covered all but his dark eyes. He was holding the longest needle I'd ever seen in my life. "Turn her on her side and hold her still," he ordered the nurse.

I moaned in agony.

Realizing that I was awake, he said, "This will hurt, but you must be brave."

"No, no, nooo!" I screamed. I passed out. Years later, I

3

realized the importance of that spinal tap. It would determine whether I was infected with polio.

I awoke, thoroughly disoriented. Why was I being pushed in a pink crib? I was a big girl—four years old! I felt like I was trapped in a cage. My crib was wheeled into a small room, empty except for overhead lights. Through a window, I could see my parents with tears in their eyes talking to the doctor. I started crying, too.

The doctor pulled his mask over his nose and mouth and stepped into the room. "Ginger, you're a very sick little girl," he told me. "You have polio. We don't know how you got this disease or where it comes from. Four other families in your town have sick family members too. We're going to keep you here and help you get better."

I couldn't move a muscle, but I yearned to race into my parents' protective arms.

The next two weeks are a blurred memory. I recall pain, excruciating pain. In an effort to offset the damaging effects of polio, my doctor ordered the "Sister Kenny Treatment" to begin. Twice a day, hot wool packs—as hot as I could stand — were applied to my back and legs, relieving some of the pain and relaxing my muscles. To this day, whenever I smell hot wool, my skin itches and my mind flips back to those early days.

"ARE any of my brothers or sisters sick?" I managed to ask toward the end of the month.

"No, you're the only one," the doctor told me.

That meant that Dick, Frankie, Donna, Bob, Mike, Charlie, and three-month-old Dominic had not come down with polio. This fact puzzled everyone. I was relieved to hear this good news and thanked God for sparing them. But what did I do to deserve this illness?

In late December, my older sisters Donna and Frankie rapped on the viewing window to get my attention. They held up gifts they had brought—Rudolph and Santa coloring books and a box of Crayola crayons. I didn't know why they hadn't come into the room, and I wondered why they came, but not my brothers?

I felt like a zoo animal. Peeking at my sisters from behind the cold bars of my crib, I felt abandoned and forsaken, but also grateful for their love and gifts. They stayed for a few minutes, until a nurse shooed them away. Blowing kisses to me, they waved goodbye. Christmastime and I was alone in this horrible place. There was nothing— no tree, no presents, no carols, no cards, no special cookies and no family. I wanted to go home to my own bed! I wanted my dog, Blackie.

With each passing day, I grew more and more bewildered about my topsy-turvy life and the pain that came with this thing called polio. After almost a month, Mom was allowed inside the isolation room—but only with a cap over her hair, a mask, and a long hospital gown. With a squeal of delight, I held out my weak arms, sure she'd pick me up and take me home. "Honey, the doctor says I can't touch you or hold you yet because of germs." I could tell it was hard for my mother, but I felt betrayed.

"I'm so happy to see you!" Mom said, coming close with hungry eyes looking me up and down, studying me carefully. My face must have revealed my deep hurt. Mom tried to be encouraging. "You're looking better! Your pretty eyes are bright and alert, and you're awake and talking to me." I could tell she was trying to convince herself as well as me.

The nurse tapped on the window and held up five fingers then pointed to her watch.

"I can't stay long, sweetheart. They won't let me," Mom

said as she acknowledged the warning from the nurse with a wave of her hand.

I whined, "Don't leave me Mommy! Growing panicky, I pleaded, "Please don't go." Gasping for air and with tears spilling down my face I wailed, "Mommy, I wanna go home!"

"There, there now, calm down and listen to me. I want you to come home too, but you have to get better. The doctor says you're improving more and more every day."

When she turned the door knob, her smile wavered. "Think happy thoughts, my brave little girl. Jesus is with you. He'll give both of us the courage we need. Say your prayers. You know I'll be praying for you. I love you. Now, hush." She sang the Irish lullaby "Too Ra Loo Ra Loo Ral." Her singing comforted me. However, when the door closed behind her, I let the tears fall.

I often heard children crying inconsolably in other rooms. But Mom's lullaby and message stayed with me, and I tried to take comfort from them. She said I was getting better and on the road to recovery. I just didn't know how long that road would be.

2

POLIO

IN THE EARLY 1950s, summertime was not a happy-go-lucky time. It was a terrifying time. Children were discouraged, even forbidden, to go to the beach or swim in community pools, or even to attend public gatherings. It was too risky. Children were also supervised in their activities so they wouldn't overexert themselves. A frightful and dangerous predator lurked nearby and no one understood who that predator was. We didn't know where or why the danger existed, but we knew about its devastation.

Why all the fuss? Infantile Paralysis was on a rampage across our country, targeting children, especially those less than five years of age. My Mom was especially concerned about baby Dominic. He wasn't even four months old yet. She had gone through a difficult pregnancy with him during the early months and had to take frequent rest times. She considered him to be the most vulnerable. Adults were not entirely exempt either. In time, the virus became known by the more common and dreaded name of polio.

I didn't get sick in the summer like many other children. I was rushed to the hospital in late November of 1950.

News media gave daily reports of the scourge. In 1952, the United States reported over 57,000 polio cases—one of the worst U.S. epidemics on record. Approximately one out of a hundred cases resulted in paralysis. The other victims recovered in a week or two, exhibiting only flu-like symptoms. In my hometown of Dexter, Michigan, four people contracted polio when I did. One child died.

The history of polio can be traced back two thousand years or more. Egyptian records show paintings and carvings of humans ravaged by polio. In the United States, polio reached its peak between 1949 and 1953, when indoor plumbing became standard. Before this time, when sanitation conditions were poor, children built up a natural immunity to the disease and polio was relatively rare. Early television programs brought the "soap stories" along with their advertisements promoting products like Twenty Mule Team Borax, Roman Cleanser, and Ivory Soap. Americans became more cleanliness-conscious in hopes of keeping diseases from their doors. Ironically, the cleaner we got as a nation, the more resistant the polio virus became.

After many long studies, researchers discovered that polio is contracted through the mouth. When it enters the gastrointestinal tract, it causes flu-like symptoms. For many, it was a benign illness. Their bodies fought it off. In paralytic or spinal polio, the virus caused additional symptoms, including severe headaches, a stiff neck, and rapid paralysis as the nerve axons connecting the anterior horn cells of the spinal column to the muscles were killed. During this acute stage, patients were most vulnerable. Bulbar polio affected the gray matter of the brain, causing paralysis of the muscles used in breathing and swallowing. Those who caught both the paralytic and bulbar polio couldn't breathe on their own. They were placed in iron lungs and seldom lived over a year. No two polio cases were exactly alike. However, people with polio share common problems and treatments.

In the early 1940's, Dr. Jonas Salk did the initial work on the polio vaccine in Ann Arbor before leaving for Pittsburgh in 1947. Later, the University of Michigan was selected as the center of field trials for the Salk vaccine. In 1955, ten years after the death of polio's most well-known victim, President Franklin D. Roosevelt, the world finally had its first polio vaccine.

ALONE AND AFRAID IN A SCARY WORLD

I DID NOT DIE in Contagious Hospital. During the first week of the new year, I was transferred to Ten East on the children's polio floor of the University of Michigan Hospital in Ann Arbor. Tony, a good-humored transporter, wheeled me there on a stretcher. When we reached a crowd in the hall, he pulled me onto the neighboring ward, Ten West. As I looked down that wing, tears stung my eyes like bees. I saw children with their whole bodies inserted into giant tin cans. Only their heads stuck out. "What's the matter with those kids?" My voice quivered when I asked the question. "What's that strange whooshing sound?"

"Those machines, called iron lungs, are helping them breathe."

The face of one boy still haunts my dreams. His eyes were reflected in the viewing mirror that hung over his head and they were filled with grief. I tried to smile, but it hurt to smile. I waved instead.

"Tony, am I like them?" I felt very brave when I asked.

"Nope. You're lucky to have good healthy lungs," he said reassuringly.

In Ten East, Mom greeted me while Tony moved me off the stretcher and into a real bed—even if it was a hospital bed and not my at-home bed. Mom introduced me to my three roommates. Sally had freckles and long blond braids. Maggie had short black hair and a shy smile. Blossom, resting in her bed on her back in the far corner, flashed a cheerful smile. Her Caribbean blue eyes sparkled and wild red curls crowned her head. These girls, like me, looked like they had come through a polio storm with the wind knocked out of their sails, adrift on a choppy sea. I was happy to be with young people who understood what was happening to me, but I was especially glad to have my mom by my side. It was a short-lived joy, however. Nurse Mullins ordered, "It's time to go, Mrs. Visel."

Mom reached into her purse and pulled out a small bottle of Halo shampoo. "Sometime tomorrow, could someone please shampoo and cut my little girl's hair? It's been so long since she's had it washed properly."

"Mrs. Visel, I promise I'll do my best," Nurse Mullins sighed.

The next morning, I discovered that a shampoo was no easy task. I was rolled onto a stretcher and pushed into a dingy cubbyhole that had a large tub with a hose and shower nozzle. I was told to scoot up until my head hung over the end of the stretcher. The kind nurse washed my hair squeaky clean while singing the advertising jingle. "Halo, everybody, Halo. Halo is the shampoo that glorifies your hair so. Halo shampoo, Halo."

Laughing, she toweled my hair. "Now hold your head up. Lean on your elbows." She picked up a big pair of shears and finished the job. My new hairdo was fluffy and light. I liked how I smelled clean. I gave her a big hug and together we sang the jingle on our way back to my room. There we met Tony, who announced he'd be taking me to physical therapy.

"You probably don't recognize the glamorous Miss Visel," Nurse Mullins said, smiling.

"No," Tony responded. "I thought she was a movie star!"

On the way, Tony told me I was done with the hot pack treatments. "The doctors want you in the Hubbard Tank twice a week. You're going to get movie star treatments," he chuckled.

"What's that mean?" I asked.

"It's like a big tub of water. It'll make you feel good. You'll love it."

Hydrotherapy is a treatment used in physical therapy that became popular in America immediately after World War II. Federal agencies supported research, education, and development in orthotics and prosthetics for many veterans. In case after case, hydrotherapy proved to be a crucial component in their initial rehabilitation. Patients were lowered into a large hot water tub called a Hubbard Tank, whose pulsating jets provided a warm water massage that helped to stimulate blood circulation and relieve pain. The Hubbard Tank offered the same benefit to polio victims whose rigid limbs needed massage and stimulation too, especially for flexibility. At the same time, it helped keep the muscles from growing weaker. Here again, heat was one of the key factors for relaxing muscles, similar to the Sister Kenny Treatment.

I was now considered a survivor...a very wounded and depleted one. At this stage, in the main hospital, I was transported on a stretcher whenever I left my room for therapy or anything else. My arms ached. I was unable to sit up on my own and was shaky and weak. It was a struggle to turn on my side. If I wanted to bend my legs, I had to use my arms and hands to accomplish this small feat. My legs were rigid and paralyzed. The only traces of movement occurred in my toes. The right toes could wiggle up and down, but the left toes could just go downward. Headaches still came and went. I was most comfortable propped up with a pillow when they would allow it. Just being awake and trying to get into some kind of a daily routine was exhausting. I felt nothing like my old self.

The elevator clunked to a stop on the ground floor. The elevator operator pulled back the inside folding door and the outer door opened. Exposed pipes hissed and bellowed overhead all the way down a long, dingy corridor to the physical therapy section. It reeked of chlorine. "Try to be a good little soldier," Tony said.

I didn't want to be a soldier. I wanted to be a movie star.

The physiotherapist eased me into the tank on a body sling, sinking me up to my chin in the warm churning water. For a moment, I thought I might drown, but I soon felt the water massage my muscles. It made my arms and legs feel good. I wondered if this is what it felt like when a canoe got caught in the rapids in the river. I didn't want the bath to end. I protested when the sling slowly raised me out of the tank and I felt the cold air quickly cooling down my hot body. My body tingled all over and my skin looked sunburned. "That felt great," I gasped.

When Tony reappeared, he said cheerfully, "Okay, young lady, we have one more appointment for you this morning. We're off to the appliance shop." We traded the smell of chlorine for the smells of leather, oil, and sweat. When I was wheeled into this department, I saw an older woman sitting at the desk chewing gum. "Come on in, honey," she said in a Southern accent. She called back to the shop area, saying, "Jim, your eleven o'clock is here." Then she went back to her typing.

Jim turned out to be a short man with big muscles and brown hair. Quietly he explained, "I'm going to build you a nighttime appliance to help your feet grow right." After he measured my legs and feet, he slipped socks and a new pair of white high-top shoes on my feet. "How are they?"

"Gee, I never wore shoes like that," I answered.

Pulling a black marker from his apron pocket, he felt for the spot where my toes began. He drew a line on each shoe there before taking them off. "Don't go away, I'll be right back."

I opened my eyes wide and then realized he was making a joke. When he returned, he put the shoes back on. He had cut off the top part, and my toes stuck out! Straightening my legs and spacing them about twelve inches apart, he bolted a metal bar to the bottom of the shoes. "The doctors want you to wear this at night," he explained.

"Noooo!" I howled. I wanted to kick that awful thing away.

Jim winced. "You need to cooperate. Your doctors know best." In an effort to soften the blow, he added, "It won't be forever."

BACK ON THE POLIO FLOOR, the lunch carts were making their way down the hall. Lunch time was followed by a mandatory rest period. With all the morning activity, I had no trouble taking a nap. It's a good thing I didn't have to wear the new foot appliance during the afternoon rest period.

The weekday visiting hours were from 3 to 4 p.m. Weekend hours were 3 to 5 p.m. Only grown-up relatives were allowed to visit. The Galen Society Ladies, dressed in coral smocks, were available to chat, loan books, or play a game with children who did not have a visitor. I looked longingly at their book carts full of picture books and the toy cart that held dolls just waiting to be hugged. Most of us had only one special toy or doll of our own. One of the ladies read me *The Little Red Hen* and loaned it to me. "Thank you," I said, remembering my manners. "This book makes me happy. I think it's good medicine."

"And how is that?" she asked me with a curious look.

"Well, the Little Red Hen didn't give up when no one would help her. She worked hard and made yummy bread for herself and her chicks."

The lady laughed and patted my hand saying, "If you want something, Ginger, work hard for it."

Toward evening the janitor swept and wet-mopped the floor and emptied the litter baskets. Aides brought fresh pitchers of ice water and bedtime snacks of fruit juices and peanut butter crackers. At 8:00 p.m., hall lights were dimmed and the ward grew quiet. Only the nightlights over each bed broke the darkness.

Just as casually as can be, the night shift nurse made her rounds with a chart asking each patient, in an embarrassingly loud voice, "Did you have a bowel movement today?" If you said, "Yes," she'd ask, "Was it a soft stool or a solid stool?" It was awful to have to answer that question day after day.

I was afraid of the dark, especially when sleeping alone. At home, I always slept between my brothers Charlie and Mike. I didn't have anyone to whisper to or giggle with under the covers. No bedtime story either. No parent to tuck me in and hear my prayers. No goodnight kiss. No lullaby. Just a lot of sick children in a lot of pain, away from home. The night was filled with heartrending cries.

I had to sleep on my back without a pillow, because doctors thought this might keep my spine from curving. Now I also had a torturous device to add to my agonizing nights. The nurse strapped on the high-top shoes fastened to the steel bar. This awful contraption hurt me. Through horrible long hours, the nurses frantically tried to make me feel better. I rolled my head from side to side, hoping if I got dizzy enough, I could sleep.

Nighttime was crying time. During the day when strangers came and went away from my bed I could tuck my fears, pain, and confusion deep inside. I tried to do what Mommy told me, hoping that, if I was good enough, I could leave this bad place and go home. However, in the shadows of the night, I burrowed under the sheet and let the tears spill when no one was there to see. I often felt so desperately alone and afraid in a scary world. This was one of those nights.

Sometime around midnight, a nurse, whom I will always regard as my angel of mercy, heard me whimpering. She didn't poke me with a needle, put a cold metal thing on my chest, or stick a thermometer in my bottom. Instead, she said, "You've worn this thing long enough for one night," and took the appliance off my aching feet. Then she turned me over, squirted lotion in her hands, and gave me a soothing backrub. Her warm hands massaging my back were a treat. To be touched in such a comforting way soon put me into a deep sleep.

IN JANUARY, I gradually felt stronger, especially in my upper body. I could sit up without getting tired. My life was coming back to me. I felt I was living in a four-year-old's real time, not in some feverish, foggy world. That's when I realized a hospital is not as sterile and clean as grownups think. The air was full of yucky smells from bedpans, bloody bandages, and sweat. I gasped and longed for a breath of fresh air. Now, all these years later, I cringe at the thought that at the end of the week, I did something that made another nighttime problem.

Our room call light had been on for a very long and

uncomfortable time. My roommates had gone to sleep. I wanted to go to sleep too. But I needed to use the bedpan. I couldn't hold out much longer. I wanted to cry. I had a stomach ache. My body started fighting to stay in control. I was more than half past four. Soon I'd be five! I was too big to poop my pants. *Whoops!* Nature took its course.

Mortified, I reached for some Kleenex. Slowly, carefully, I peeled off my thick cotton underpants. At least the smell of this one wasn't bad, I tried to reassure myself. Covering the poop with tissues and folding the material and contents into a tight wad, I threw the bundle across the room, hoping it would land in the wastebasket. But it didn't. It plopped down on the floor next to the wastebasket. At least it was off of me and away from my bed, but there was no way I could retrieve it. My legs had forgotten how to use their "go power." I couldn't even raise my toes on my left foot. I had to use my arms if I wanted to move my legs. I struggled to stand. And if I managed that with someone's help, I had to hold on to something or someone to steady myself. Otherwise, I would collapse into a heap. The simple ability to walk, jump, skip, and run had been stolen from me. My body felt like a wet noodle.

Relieved, I wrapped the sheet around myself like a mummy. No sooner had I done that, when Nurse Mullins popped her head through the doorway, quietly asking, "Does someone need help?" My face got as red as the fall apples on the tree in our backyard, and my body felt hot and sweaty. Holding my breath, I was terrified to confess and scared to tell a lie. I thought if I kept pretending to sleep, she'd go away.

When she beamed her flashlight in my direction, I froze in place like I imagined a criminal would. The minutes stretched out painfully until the light came to rest on the bundle by the wastebasket. Cautiously walking over there, she halted when she detected a whiff of my business. "Oh, what Little Scuttlebutt pulled this nasty trick?" she snarled. "Lord, have mercy!" Shaking her head, she picked up the dirty evidence between two fingers. Holding it away from herself, she huffed out the door.

All I could think of was my mother, and how much I missed her.

———————

BY MID-JANUARY, my orthopedic doctor started visiting me during early morning rounds surrounded by men in short white coats he called his medical students. "How are you doing?" he'd ask me. I didn't like having strangers talk about me and point and ask me nosey questions.

Looking back, I realize I felt like a laboratory specimen during these trying times. Those men looked at me as if I were a dead cat or a frog, analyzing me and listing me in their files as another case study. It's as if *Ginger*, the person, wasn't there. What was even more nerve-wracking was that they never explained anything to me in plain English. All I knew was that I hurt all over and couldn't move much, my parents were kept away from me, and people could poke and prod and stick needles into me. They treated me like a bad rubber doll, not a little girl with a heart and homesickness. Mostly, I was filled with fear. "Just take it one day at a time, and be thankful for the small gains I see you making," Mom would tell me.

And I did make small gains.

When the doctor and his team left and the breakfast trays were collected, I gave myself a bed-bath every day. An aide washed my back. I was expected to get dressed. "No more hospital gowns," Nurse Mullins announced. Every day I chose either a plaid or striped dress from the clothes cart. These oversized dresses were starched, with short puffy sleeves and were tied into a bow at the back. I wore white cotton socks to help keep my feet warm. In time, I learned to transfer myself into the wooden-slat wheelchair that an aide pulled to the bed. "You need to do all of this if you want to return to the real world," she explained.

In the physical therapy department, Dr. Koepke was "The General" and Miss Johnstone was "The Sergeant." I noticed the big gold badge sewn to the sleeve of her uniform and was impressed, thinking it was for her high rank. After my examination, Dr. Koepke told me he had an appointment with my Mom. "Be good and don't give Sergeant any problems," he said, leaving the room.

I wondered why everyone said that. Wasn't I good? Was that why I got polio, because I was bad?

What did I do to "deserve" polio? I never injured anybody or hurt anyone with bad words. I tried to do good things to make others happy. I'd pick wild flowers and put them in a vase to make our dinner table pretty. And I could set the table for dinner, too. I colored animal pictures to hang on the kitchen cupboards and played with my little brother Charlie who was one year younger than me. Mommy always told me I was "a good little helper."

I thought about what I might have done wrong and couldn't think of hardly anything. But I knew Charlie was naughty on liver and onions night. He'd pass off half of his liver under the table to Blackie when Mom and Dad weren't looking and pretended that he cleaned his plate just fine. Mike, who was older, did all kinds of mean things to Charlie and me—like scaring us with awful stories about The Boogie Man that's "going to get you if you don't watch out!"

I never told anyone, but I always thought of The Boogie Man as the polio stalker who lurked around trying to bring me down again. Sometimes Mike would sneak a flashlight out of the drawer downstairs and hide it under his pillow. When he thought we were all cozy and snuggly and almost asleep, he'd start making eerie sounds and hold his hand over the light as he shined it on the wall making his hand a giant shadow reaching down to grab us—scaring the heck out of Charlie and me who had to share a bed with him. He was terrible.

Bob was trouble too, on occasion, but not to us. Last August, before I got polio, he and a friend pulled a prank on a neighboring farmer. They got caught stealing watermelons. The farmer was doing some late-night work in his barn and was going up to his house when he happened to spy them messing around in his watermelon patch. When Dad found out about it, Bob had to apologize to the farmer and do chores for him for a week to work off the damage and learn a lesson.

On the other hand, my sister Donna, who was seven years older than me, hadn't done anything bad that I could remember. Frankie was a year older than Donna. The two of them got along just fine. But Frankie had a temper and our oldest brother Dick hassled her from time to time and called her names. When she got really mad, she'd throw something. And, she was often intolerant with us little folks. And Dick wasn't always a saint. Some Saturday nights he partied a little too much and Dad had to get on his case as well. None of them got polio. Only me.

The Sergeant got back to me and stretched me and worked my legs. To reward me, she gave my back a great massage. She made me feel good and safe. Back in the rickety wooden wheelchair, I rolled along the hallway to Dr. Koepke's office. "Miss Johnstone, will I ever see you again?" I asked.

Her answer made me wonder about things to come. "Oh, we'll be seeing a lot of each other, Miss Ginger. You can count on that!"

The doctor's door was partially open. Quiet as a mouse, I wheeled closer, hoping to get a peek at Mom. He was doing most of the talking—about how bad my legs were deteriorating. When he saw Mom's tears, he said, "We're going to do all we can, even surgeries, but there's a strong possibility that your daughter may never walk again. After all, there's not much you can do with a burnt-out light bulb."

Surgeries? Hospitalized, flesh opened under the knife, stitched closed and scarred for life, legs encased in heavy casts, resigned to tons of incredible pain. Never stand? Never walk? Never run or jump? Never dance? People threw away their burnt-out light bulbs. Would my family forget about me? They had so many other children to take care of, after all.

"She'll walk," Mom contradicted.

My heart seemed to grow a hundred times bigger. I secretly promised, "My light will shine again, Mom."

Mom smiled in relief when she saw me up and about in a wheelchair. "Come on, we're going to celebrate. We can splurge once in a while."

It had been over two weeks since her last visit. To my surprise, she wheeled me to the hospital store and she bought great treats—an Almond Joy candy bar, Juicy Fruit gum, and *Little Girl Paper Dolls!* Even at my age, I understood that with our big family, money was tight, so that meant a lot.

We found a phone. Mom helped me to drop a dime into the slot. "You tell me our number and I'll dial."

I gave her the number clearly. She talked to Dad, and then handed me the phone. I was so happy to hear his voice and to speak with two of my brothers for a few precious minutes. Mike wanted to know, "Do you have a room of your own?"

And Charlie excitedly said, "It snowed. Me and Mike made a fat snowman."

The hardest part of being away from home was being

isolated from my family. Sometimes I worried that they'd forget all about me, especially with our latest addition, baby brother Dominic. I was already missing out on him trying to take his first steps.

Before she left, Mom took me to a quiet place at the end of a long corridor she called the hospital chapel. She opened the big door and we entered. A few older patients in hospital bathrobes sat in the semi darkness along with a couple of other adults. Vigil candles flickered with a soft glow in their red, blue or gold containers and yellow roses graced the altar. "Wow Mom, I never knew this place existed. This is like a little church. Why is it in this big hospital?"

"It's for people like you and me who want to talk to God and have a little peace and quiet. I stop in here after each time I visit you and pray to God to watch over you, to protect you, and to help you get better so you can come home." She rolled my wheelchair over to the end of a pew and sat in a seat beside me and held my hand.

After praying, Mom promised to do everything she could to help me walk. "Ginger, do you know what a pact is? It's a trade or agreement. I made a pact with God that I would quit smoking if He would help me help you get better."

By her example she taught me to believe, "With God all things are possible." I was an obedient child and did as my Mom suggested. When I felt weepy, I'd think of my family and the good times we shared together and what they might be doing at any given moment. I said my prayers in the morning to begin the day and night prayers to end it. I said before and after meal prayers. I also prayed for the sick kids around me and my doctors, nurses and all the hospital helpers. I began to feel the love and presence of Jesus by my side and was learning the virtue of self-control. I didn't have to focus on feeling sorry for myself and making others miserable with temper tantrums and being grouchy and crying constantly. By staying in touch with Jesus, He helped to steady me.

WOULD I EVER GO HOME?

In February, the doctors continued to prescribe hydrotherapy for me three days a week. The other two days, I had table exercises with Miss Johnstone followed by back and leg massage. Tony took me to the Appliance Shop where Jim fit me for leg braces. My stomach flip-flopped and my spirits dropped when I heard that the night shoe torture wouldn't be enough. They wanted me in leg braces during the day.

However, the next day I was in for a surprise. Nurse Mullins chirped, "Ginger, you can start going to school two or three times a week. Your doctor thinks you've made some good progress and that you're well enough to get off the floor to study and play with other children. Besides, you need a change of atmosphere. It will help cheer you up." Tony wheeled me to the thirteenth floor, where I found the school. On the roof! "When it's warm you can go outside onto the small sun porch," he said.

"You mean I'll still be here then?" My heart sank. I didn't think I would ever go home.

The school was one great room sprinkled with patients on stretchers, in beds, and in wheelchairs. I saw them all busy working with volunteer helpers. Small kids were playing with puppets, working puzzles, and studying picture books in a corner nook on small-sized furniture. Bright potted geraniums lined the window sills and a big bunny called Snowball hopped around freely.

I felt happy here.

"This is Sunny, your teacher," Tony said.

Sunny bubbled over with cheer. She gave me a lump of clay and said I could make a bowl for my Dad. "I'll fire this in the kiln, and then you can have it back," she promised. In the days to come, she offered to teach me to read and write.

"Yes!" I told her eagerly. And, indeed I did learn to read text from her mega-size, flip-chart stories about Sally, Dick, Jane, their dog named Spot, and their cat named Puff.

All too soon, it was time to go back to my dull hospital room. I'd close my eyes and vividly remember the diorama with the tiny replicas of Eskimo people by the elevator next to the hospital school. I wanted to crawl inside this other world filled with new adventures. Here, bears carved from ivory roamed the miniature wilderness. I was a witness to exotic village life, complete with igloos, sled dogs, children playing, an Indian in a kayak holding his harpoon, and women cleaning fish near a totem pole. Nearby on display was an authentic child-sized Eskimo coat with a fur hood and a pair of boots. How I longed to slip into that coat and boots and escape from the hospital world into an imaginary world without sickness and pain.

By the second week of February, Jim had crafted my leg supports and fitted me with two full-length leg braces, wooden underarm crutches, and orthopedic shoes. The left shoe had to have a one inch lift because my left leg was now shorter than my right. "The left brace locks at the knee with double locks that can be released manually when you change into a sitting position," Jim said. I would learn what these big words meant.

Jim helped to get me onto the examination table and proceeded to slip the ice-cold steel contraptions onto my legs one at a time. Each was anchored to a leather thigh band, and calf band that had leather straps that buckled and held my legs in place. A special leather knee pad covered each knee that had straps with buckles. They held my knees in place. He fitted them nice and tight. At the ankle, my feet had another strap that buckled the foot in place as well. Leather, Buster Brown orthopedic shoes with a steel shank were attached to metal ankle joints which in turn were attached to the shoes.

Jim laced my shoes and tied them tight. Miss Johnstone was ready and waiting for me when Jim pulled back the curtain around the exam table. She and Jim lifted me off the table and into the wheelchair. I had to manually unlock the knee-locks for the first time so my leg would bend and I could sit properly. She rolled me to the parallel bars in a room with floor-to-ceiling mirrors and floor mats. She slipped a belt around my waist and pulled it tight. "All right now, I promise I won't let you get hurt. I'm going to help you stand and walk."

"No-o-o!" I moaned. "How am I supposed to walk in these heavy things?" Each brace with an attached shoe weighed a couple of pounds and I was just a little girl. Add the klutzy crutches to the mix that made my arms ache. I didn't have to dig down far to know how angry I was in that moment because of what polio had done to me. I'd already had to surrender so much, but I didn't want to stay stuck, parked in a wheelchair for the rest of my life. I had to keep moving forward if I ever wanted to get the heck out of this hospital and play in the fresh air again.

First, I practiced bearing weight by grabbing hold of the parallel bars and standing. Miss Johnstone demonstrated what she expected me to do. Then, taking the belt so I wouldn't fall, she got behind me and used her right knee to help push my right leg forward. Then she repeated the same thing with the left leg. That was my first step since contracting polio last November.

Slowly, step-by-step, back and forth from one end to the other, I moved as Miss Johnstone poured out encouragement. But it was not without great struggle. Trying to move with heavy braces on was exhausting work.

I had to literally swing my left leg from the hip since I had to walk stiff-legged with my left leg. I had to pause and breathe deeply after each step. I grew hot and sweaty. I moved slower than a snail as I focused hard on each movement. Later I learned that I was biting my lip without noticing it in my concentration, and it was bleeding.

After weeks of practice, Miss Johnstone expected me to practice on my own while she worked with other patients. Often, without the belt, I fell. "That's what the mats are for," she said matter-of-factly. I remember the physical and emotional pain, and how I struggled to get back up and work until the end of the session. Looking back on those difficult days, I think of myself as the Tin Man in *The Wizard of Oz*.

I also recall Burl Ives' song "The Little Engine That Could." The little blue engine with the great big load tells himself over and over again, "I can do most anything if I only think I can." When he huffs and puffs up the mountain to deliver the goods, he sings, "I knew I could, I knew I could, I knew I could." I frequently remembered that song as I tried to be like the brave little blue engine.

Full-length braces made with steel, buckles, and leather straps left track marks on my skin as much as they did on my soul. Custom-made as I grew to correct the peculiarities left by polio, they required several fittings to fine-tune them. And then it would take weeks to break them in.

If parts of my body didn't comply, there were consequences. My left baby toe suffered through generations of corns as it twisted sideways. Nobody paid attention to it when I complained. They never straightened it in surgery. My puny left leg never caught up to my right leg, forcing me to limp, which added pressure on my big toe and caused another corn. My nightly routine included an application of Freezone to the corns for two weeks before they fell off, similar to the procedure for removing a wart.

Relief was short-lived. Blisters, bruises, and rashes erupted, too. I learned to shift positions, propping my foot on a stool when sitting, and practiced coping techniques to handle pain. Mind over matter. Once, when I whined about having to go into the appliance shop to have worn parts replaced on my braces, Mom reprimanded me, "You ought to be glad you're able to wear them out."

As THE DAYS went by without seeing my family, the long hours grew heavy with loneliness and disappointment. Plus, a visitor might take you to the sunroom, or at least push you down the hallway to have a different view. My roommate, Blossom, must have felt like this when she was stuck in bed all the time and hardly ever got to leave our room.

I breathed in sadness that seemed to hover around my hospital bed like secondary smoke. I tried to wave it away, but it hit me right in my face. Depression, plus exhaustive physical therapy, made me feel stretched like a guitar string ready to snap. And I was so uncomfortable that I couldn't sleep.

On one particular day, all I could think of was to pray my simple child's prayer quietly, "Jesus, help me," over and over again. When I looked up, I saw Father Walsh standing in the doorway in his black robe. His sympathetic eyes peered through his gold spectacles. Taking off his tri-corner clerical hat, he put a yellow box on the bedside stand. "I just wanted to let you know a lot of people miss you and are praying for you. Jesus hears your prayers and is with you."

My head hurt so badly that his words sounded fuzzy. He laid his cool hand on my head, said some prayers, and left me with his blessing. I slept through the night for the first time.

All was quiet in the overheated hospital room the next morning, except for the hiss and dull knock of the radiator on the sidewall. I felt a lot better after a good night's rest. The pain was gone. For a moment, I shut my eyes tightly, wishing that I would find myself at home in bed between my little brother Charlie and my big brother Mike. Cracking an eye, my attention was soon drawn to the dandelion-yellow box on top of the bedstand. Chocolates!

It wasn't a dream. Father Walsh really had visited yesterday. I could hardly wait to tell my parents. They admired him and had even named my brother Charlie after him.

The last summer I could run on my legs, I'd had a chance to go with Dad to the grotto, modeled after the one in Lourdes, that Father Walsh had constructed on the parish grounds. We found Father at his workbench, outfitted in pants with suspenders, an old shirt with rolled-up sleeves, and a straw hat. He was whistling while putting a multi-colored glass roof on a birdhouse. He carefully chose chips of broken glass from wooden boxes. He had light green from Coca-Cola bottles, green from Vicks VapoRub jars, dark blue from Noxema jars, yellow from broken dishes, brown glass from beer bottles, and pieces of a mirror.

Father had taken broken and damaged goods and turned them into something whole and beautiful. He did the same with broken and damaged people, encouraging those broken in spirit to grow in the faith. I was one of the damaged people Father helped fix. His visits were more special than even his delicious box of chocolates.

ONCE IN A GREAT while Dad came to visit. He had to work long hours at a factory to provide for our large family, so his visits were rare. And he hated hospitals. However, in early

March, before heading to the afternoon shift a few blocks away at the Hoover Ball and Bearing Company, he managed a visit. He was dressed in his red-and-black checked coat, T-shirt, and work pants. His thick hair was slicked back with Vitalis and he was freshly shaven. When he bent down to kiss me I could smell his Old Spice cologne. How I loved that smell.

Dad reported on events back home—things that made me smile. Then he told me a story. "There was a thick fog driving back home from town yesterday morning when I stopped off at Grandma's. It was a surprise to see wild turkeys under her oak trees. What do you think they were eating?"

"Acorns!"

"You got it." Reaching into his right pocket, he found a handful of acorns with their brown caps firmly attached and sat them on the nightstand. "I picked these up for you."

I giggled. "I'm not going to eat those!"

He laughed, but then he grew serious. "Those giant oaks in Grandma's yard grew from tiny acorns just like these, and oaks are the strongest trees. If you do what everyone here tells you to do, you'll grow strong too, just like these acorns."

"Daddy, you know I'm trying awfully hard to be good and do all the things the medical people ask me to do, I promise. And I am getting better a little bit at a time." For a minute, I couldn't help thinking about Blossom. Why did she deserve to get polio so bad that she couldn't even sit up? She had to have another operation and would be stuck in bed for another nine months. What could she possibly have done that was so terrible? I hoped the doctor didn't ever have to operate on my spine.

I worried about the kids in those awful iron-lungs on the other ward too, and little Johnny down the hall. His right arm and leg were paralyzed and now he'd never realize his dream of being a baseball player. He was so sad. Everywhere I looked I saw kids with different kinds of polio problems and none of us were exactly right. What did we do to deserve having our bodies wrecked by polio? What did we do? I wished this question would stop haunting me.

Dad fished inside another pocket and found four shiny steel ball bearings. Three were the size of regular marbles. The fourth was the size of a shooter marble. "You keep these to remind you that I'm working just down the road from the hospital and I'll be thinking about you, Ginger Girl." From that day onwards, to those who spotted these shiny balls on my nightstand I proudly explained, "My Dad makes them."

My life on Ten East seemed an endless menu of boredom, physical therapy, the appliance shop, and school, served always with pain and homesickness, yet, gradually, changes became noticeable. When bunnies, chicks, and spring flowers were painted on windows, decorating the nursing station to welcome in spring, Tony wheeled me to school beside Ruby. The craft for that day was extra special. We could make a beautiful bouquet.

Ruby and I shared the scissors and other materials while we talked about our families and arranged daffodils, tulips, and pussy willows for our mothers. After a special movie about the earth, animals and birds waking up and welcoming the warm season, Ruby endearingly reached for my hand and placed it on her shiny ebony cheek, saying, "You're my friend."

This was the first time a black person had ever touched me. Opportunities to interact with people of different races were not available in my hometown. At almost five years of age I began growing in my understanding of the outside world.

The last Friday of March ended on a sad note. One of

my roommates, seven-year-old Blossom, went for a repeat spinal surgery early in the morning. All day long, I worried. Blossom didn't appear. Tears burned my eyes when the terror of the evening set in and she still hadn't returned to the room. When the night nurse made her rounds, I asked with a stomach ache, "Where's Blossom?"

She replied sadly, "Oh, honey, didn't anyone tell you? She passed away." Blossom's death sent me reeling into a pit of fear. Would I die, too? Blossom had been a cute girl with a peppy personality. She died on the operating table after having repeated spinal fusions because her back kept breaking. Each surgery had required a body cast for nine months. This time her little heart had just given out.

After her death, gray shadows seemed to hover in the halls and rooms. Everyone grew silent. The staff became numb, but tried to go about their business as usual. I had never known any person who died. Over and over, I worried about my fate. I sobbed, wishing someone from home were here to hold me.

DURING THE NEXT FEW WEEKS, I worried about money, too. How were Mom and Dad paying their bills? Were we all going to end up in the poor house because of all the expense it must take to keep me here? My family was not poor, but we sure weren't rich. I'd been in the hospital for a bunch of holidays including Christmas, New Years, Valentine's Day, and St. Patrick's Day. But I missed Donna's February birthday, also. Now it was my birthday and next week was the Easter holiday and I would miss my Moms' birthday celebration, too. Everybody is supposed to be home for the holidays, not stuck in a hot stuffy hospital. I wanted to go outside in the nice spring weather and play. I felt like I was stuck in a trap and couldn't do anything about it.

When Mom came to visit a short time later and heard my distress, she told me not to worry my silly head about bills. She said God was looking out for us. In the first place this was a teaching hospital where men studied to be doctors to learn how to treat polio patients. Also she explained how the whole country was collecting dimes through a charity known as The March of Dimes. Good people all over the country were contributing to the fight against polio. Part of that money went to help rehabilitate people like me, who have polio, and to search for a safe vaccine.

Mom said, "I have a surprise for you. I didn't come here to talk about bills and money. It's your fifth birthday on a sunny afternoon. Let's go over here and look out the window at this glorious sunny day." I had a heart-clutching moment when Mom picked me up to look out the window and I spied my brothers and sisters ten floors below! They were all there. Dick, the oldest, was fifteen. Dominic, the youngest, was almost one. They looked like tiny elves as they romped far below on the lawn. My sisters were doing cartwheels and my brothers were playing tackle football and trying to make me laugh.

Healthy children were not allowed on the ward, even for special occasions. I loved seeing them, but hated the distance between us. Their visit was a wonderful birthday gift. But, I wondered, did they miss me as much as I missed them? Did they count the weeks and months I'd been away like I did? A long sigh rose up from my toes as I wished I was able to spring free from this place to run and tumble with them in the fresh, sweet-smelling grass.

The following week was Easter Sunday. I awoke to find a curious and colorful cloth bag at the bottom of my bed. Inside I found a cute monkey puppet, a child's apron, a

Little Golden Book, a dot-to-dot coloring book, and a pink octopus with braided arms and pastel colored hair-ribbons. The Easter Bunny had found me at the hospital.

I received another very special Easter gift the next day when Dr. Koepke asked me, "What would you say if I told you that you're going to be going home at the end of the month?"

4

FIND A HAPPY PLACE

FINALLY, at the end of April, I was released from the hospital in full-length leg braces and crutches. Raising my chin and holding back the tears, I refused the wheelchair. I stood my ground.

I struggled to the car resolving to someday even dance again. Soon, I was back at home! But I didn't feel happy inside. Things were weird. My older siblings, who used to kid around and hug and tickle me, now kept their distance. They acted cautious around me, even stand-offish. After such long, clinical, painful months I wanted to be cuddled. Their behavior perplexed me. Twelve-year-old Donna helped me understand this puzzle. She said, "I don't want to hurt you. Neither does anyone else."

The adjustment period took time for all of us to understand, especially Charlie, who couldn't bounce on my bed or jar me and knock me over. They needed to acclimate to my braces and my awkward movements. They tried to be quiet when I slept during the day and brought me things that I needed when I was awake. In time, Mike, who was three years older than I was, would play Candy Land with me. He loved it when my marker got stuck for a turn or two in the Molasses Swamp or when I had to go back several spaces. Sometimes we played checkers, too. I also read picture books to Charlie, who would be four in another month. Little by little, life returned to a new normal.

Mom didn't waste any time in launching our physical therapy routine. She firmly believed that role modeling was important. As soon as the older kids left for school, she'd have Charlie entertain Dominic. Then she'd turn on the television with the fourteen-inch black-and-white screen and listen to the "Jack LaLanne Show." Sometimes she had to adjust the rabbit ear antennas to get a clear picture. Mom did her thirty minutes of exercises with the exercise guru, and then she'd say, "Okay, Kiddo, it's your turn," and pop me onto the table. We did all the exercises Miss Johnstone showed us.

Mom named my legs "Lefty" (the weaker leg) and "Righty" (the stronger leg). She made up games and rhymes as a distraction from the pain as we worked together. She invented cheers when stretching my legs saying, "With a left, left, left and a right, right, right."

Then I'd lie on my back while she held my feet together and I'd do half sit-ups since I couldn't do full ones. Next, I flipped to my tummy with my arms by my side and raised my head to stretch my spine. While sitting and keeping my legs straight, I touched my nose to my knees twenty times for another spine stretch. Other stretching exercises targeted my hips and hamstrings.

Mom sent away to Jack LaLanne to buy his blue stretching band with loops on each end. It resembled a jump rope made out of rubber. I put my foot in one of the loops and raised, lowered, and stretched each leg one at a time, and did other exercises as well. Soon, I could stretch, bend easily, and do twists and turns, even the splits. I astounded my friends, my siblings, and myself. It felt great to be so limber. Doctors had also strongly suggested that swimming would help me, so Mom enrolled us at the YMCA. We went two times a week, and I loved it. When I was there, I had Mom's sole attention— a rare occasion in a family with eight children.

Mom set realistic goals. First, we worked in the shallow end of the pool, just sitting. Mom worked my legs and distracted me by singing "Little White Duck" and "Three Little Fishes." I learned to blow bubbles, duck under the water, swim like a frog, and dive to the bottom of the pool to retrieve an object while Mom also sang, "Swim, said the mama fishie, swim if you can, and they swam and they swam all over the dam."

Later, I learned to tread water and float. Then I tried swimming the width of the pool and back without touching either end. When I made that goal, I did the same with the length of the pool and back, floating part of the way. I learned to do the breast stroke, the lazy back, and the side scissor-kick. Mom turned these sessions into play times, thanks to her songs, imagination, and love.

IN JUNE OF 1951, I became an outpatient at the University of Michigan Hospital and had a morning appointment at the Bone and Joint Clinic. The cavernous waiting room looked like a furniture store, displaying sitting areas with wall-to-wall broken people, most of them in arm and leg casts or splints. The waiting room taught me thankfulness for the parts I had that worked. Patients carried their burdens on their faces and in their posture.

This is probably the first place where I realized I was being stared at. Another girl, about my age on the other side of the room, couldn't take her eyes off of me and I felt uncomfortably different. I was dressed in a dress and of course my braces were exposed. She was a stranger and probably never saw anyone in braces until now. I gave her a smile and opened a book to read thinking that if she sat over there long enough, she was going to see a lot of different appliances on a lot of people who were physically challenged.

We came prepared to sit. As Mom read me stories, I cuddled close to her. We sometimes played card games and I amused myself with paper dolls while Mom wrote her grocery list and said her rosary.

At last it was my turn. I was embarrassed when a receptionist loudly announced, "Virginia Visel." My face flushed and my heart raced when I realized all eyes were on me. Dad had named me after Mom and nicknamed me Ginger, explaining, "It fits you. Ginger is a spice made from the rootstalk of the ginger plant. It's grown as an herb in China, Africa, and India. Its flavor invigorates and adds zest to anything it's mixed with. You do that, Ginger Girl."

"Thanks Dad." I kind of liked the idea of the rootstock. Having roots gives you strength and makes you anchored. I'm glad I didn't have a nickname like my former friend, Blossom, who was frail and fragile like a real blossom and died before she had a chance to grow up. I tried to remember what Dad told me and tried to muster up some vim and vigor as I made my way into the examination room with my crutches and leg braces.

I was told to undress down to my underpants, but to leave the socks, shoes and braces on and to put on a gown that tied in the back. A transporter arrived, put me on a stretcher, and brought me into an assembly room. It was filled with about twenty doctors. I heard Dr. Carl Badgley, Professor of Surgery, tell Dr. George Koepke and my Mom, "It is critical to closely monitor the continued effects of polio on Ginger's growth and development. A group of resident doctors are joining us today." All were

male. Women weren't admitted to the program at
that time.

My doctors stood beside a life-size replica of a human
skeleton. It was as scary as the gathering. My x-rays were
displayed on a lighted screen off to the side. Even though
Mom sat on a chair right by me, I dreaded being the center
of attention. I was mortified that I had to be practically
naked and that Mom and I were the only girls there.

I had to walk for them with my crutches and braces
minus the gown. Even with the appliances, my left leg
dragged noticeably. I listened to them talk about my back.
"Note, it is beginning to be an S-curve. They talked about
me as if I were a piece of furniture. When the doctors said
they didn't know how tall I would grow, I had to fight
the tears.

Mom was five foot, eight inches tall and Dad was five
foot, eleven inches tall. "The taller the girl grows, the more
problematic balance could become," Dr. Badgley
announced. My stomach hurt. I thought of "The Little
Mermaid" and I, too, wondered if I would ever have legs
that worked. When the doctor pointed out that my left knee
buckled without warning, I snuck a glance at the solemn
expressions and furrowed brows in my audience and
wished I could race back home and hide.

Next, I was back on the stretcher and my braces were
removed. Dr. Koepke stuck a pin in both legs in different
places to check for feeling. He smiled at all positive
responses and pricked me again when I yelled, "Ouch!"
Then he measured both legs, proving my left leg was
shorter than the right.

During this era of the polio epidemic in our country
very little was known about the disease. The major focus
was where did it come from? What factors dictated who
would come down with it? And, what were the best
practices for rehabilitation? I was now in the rehabilitation

stage. It was during these sessions, which met about every three to six months, that the doctors prescribed some options to try. They wanted to keep a close eye on the patient and evaluate the pros and cons of the proposals.

Between my first three surgeries the doctors experimented with a few options. When I was at home I should try going without any braces for a couple of hours a day. This worked fine because it helped to strengthen the weaker muscles and increased blood flow. Also, I could lean on the furniture if I needed to prevent falls.

At first Dick took this to the extreme and hid my braces when I started to get weary. He thought he was doing me a favor by giving me a chance to "really build my muscles" when it actually had the opposite effect. He'd say things like, "Listen, don't you want to go to dances when you grow up?" He'd make me feel really bad. Mom and Dad had to intervene.

Another option was tried. Since I was eventually able to free my right leg from a full–length brace (which was the stronger leg to begin with), why not try putting my left leg into a short knee brace, which buckled on with a leather strap just under the knee. This did more harm than good. This leg proved to require a full-length brace in spite of much physical therapy and surgeries. It was just too weak.

I was used as a study like this about twice a year until I turned ten. Over time, I tried to develop my sense of humor to help me endure these humiliating times. I made faces at the big medical words they used and tried to find something funny to think about. If I hadn't, I would have cried. I hated being put on exhibit. I felt shamed and degraded. I wanted to hide under a blanket and disappear, even when they clapped and thanked me for being such a brave girl.

I don't think I could have survived those years without Mom. She was my cheerleader and constant support. "See the positive. Because of you, they will learn how to help other people who get polio," she said. In later years, I learned to be thankful to live so close to such a fine medical university. I was blessed to have such wonderful doctors.

Breaking out of the stuffy hospital into the bright sunshine and the warm fresh air, Mom needed to get the car out of the parking lot so I sat on the bench near the circular drive in front of the hospital facing Observatory and East Medical Drive. "It'll take about fifteen minutes, stay on the bench," she instructed. Although it was a gorgeous day, I was tired after the long morning session.

I sat sideways on the edge of the bench to catch some sun and studied the outside of University of Michigan Hospital while I waited. It was a massive building that opened in 1925. I remembered my Grandpa McGinn telling me about it one time last winter. "It's the biggest and best university-owned hospital in our country. They'll take good care of you here," he'd said. The sun highlighted the beautiful Limestone of the facade. It really was a grand building. I especially liked the fancy arch above the main entrance that was decorated with carved stone pictures of flowers and faces of important men. The seals of the state of Michigan and the University of Michigan above its decorative arch gave it a noble look.

Recalling the words of my Grandpa inspired me to whisper a prayer of thanksgiving for being able to be rehabilitated in this place. I knew deep down that the medical staff was trying to do everything possible to help me strive and thrive in my battle against polio.

Mom pulled over to the curb saying, "Chin up. I know the perfect place to eat our yummy sack lunches. It's just a stone's throw away. Hop in." She drove a short distance down a big hill to the peony garden in Nichols Arboretum. Here, we discovered the flowers in full bloom.

"Whoa! Mom, this place is so beautiful!" I sighed, as

islands of white, pink, and red peonies floated above a sea of green. We sat on a park bench midway down on the far side of the garden in the shade of a maple tree. When I raised my eyes above the garden, I could see the top of the hospital and thought to myself, "I like being down here, outside of that building, in the sunshine, rather than being on the inside of that place."

Nestled in this sacred spot, my body felt refreshed as if it had gone through a car wash, coming out shiny and clean, free of dirt and grime. At last, peace found me. I've lived my life according to Mom's next words, "When you're feeling down and out, go find a happy place. It doesn't have to be far away. You have the power to change. You just have to make up your mind and do it."

WHEN JUNE HEATED UP, Mom ended our membership at the YMCA. She applied the old Afghan proverb, "Bloom where you are planted." After all, Michigan is a water wonderland. Mom took Mike, Charlie, and me to our nearest swimming hole, in the winding 128-mile-long Huron River. From our doorstep, it was a half-mile across Dexter-Pinckney road in the front of our house, down a well-worn path, past a gurgling brook, and through a field filled with pussy willows. Part of the way, I rode piggy-back on my big brother Mike.

I needed to hold on to Mom when the steep hill slid down the slick, muddy riverbank. Often, we found tracks of a deer or a raccoon that had visited the spot before we arrived. I'd sit without braces in the cool current to get some relief from the stickiness of the midday heat. I searched for smooth river rocks and watched turtles sunning themselves on a tree limb partially submerged in the water. I stayed on the lookout for ducks or geese that fed on the duckweed, water bugs, and snails. In time, I'd take a deep breath and plunge into the brisk current for a swim.

On weekends, we piled into the family car and Dad drove us three miles to Newport Beach Club. The owners were interested in my rehabilitation and encouraged my parents to bring us all often. I loved watching Donna executing her perfect swan dive as I swam between the docks, while the juke box cranked out songs like "Love Me Tender" by Elvis Presley, "Blueberry Hill" by Fats Domino, and "Honeycomb" by Jimmy Rodgers.

5

CARRY-OUT AND SPECIAL DELIVERY

Posting myself by the window in early September 1951, I anxiously waited to hear the crunch of gravel under the tires of the yellow kindergarten bus. A few years prior to this time, the law did not allow parochial school children to ride the public school buses. My older brothers and sisters had to walk two miles to and from school for many years before our community changed the law. I was happy to ride the bus because I could never walk that far.

Mom warmly greeted Mr. Klave, the bus driver. "Your passenger is ready to go."

"Hello, Sunshine," the big burly man said, scooping me up, crutches and all, and parking me right behind the driver's seat. Smiling and chatting, he kept a close eye on me in his rear- view mirror all the way to St. Joseph Grade School. He, too, had a young daughter who had contracted polio, a much milder case than mine. Upon our arrival, he once again lifted me into his Popeye-the-Sailor-Man arms and deposited me safely inside the school saying, "You're my carry-out and special delivery kind of student. Study hard. I'll see you later."

Nineteen students were in my class. The eleven girls and eight boys were like family. Donna, along with other eighth grade girls, helped with the kindergarten class. I had learned to read in the hospital school, and now I could continue to get extra reading practice with a special eighth grade tutor. I was proud of my big sister.

At school, the stairways and hallways were monitored by the Sisters of the Immaculate Heart of Mary. They trained students to walk on one side of the hallway in an orderly fashion. I never remember being run over, pushed, or shoved. But I still worried about slipping or being bumped accidentally and losing my balance. I learned hallways could be dangerous when snow or rain was tracked in, and especially after the janitor had washed and waxed the floor, even if the floor was perfectly dry. Once, I looked like Bambi when he first went on the ice with his friend Thumper, slipping, sliding, and doing splits. From that time on, I hugged the wall or clung to someone's arm until I reached the classroom.

A bruise or a sore tailbone hurts after a fall, but what inflicted the worst pain was embarrassment. One of the worst falls occurred when the metal bar that locked my left knee broke in two. My support system caved in so fast that my head hit the floor and I saw stars. There was no permanent damage, but I had to rely on crutches full time until the brace lock got repaired.

I learned to keep my braces oiled so they wouldn't squeak and call attention to themselves. Braces can have an annoying loud squeak with each step if their joints get wet. Although it's upsetting and embarrassing, making a joke of it, something like, "Oh that's just my pet cricket chirping in my pocket!" lightened the mood.

"Polio feet," became another problem. My feet often remain ice-cold, even in a seventy- degree room. Polio attacks the nervous system, and it damaged my wiring. It also damaged my circulation system, causing purplish-blue feet. According to my brothers in the trades, they said, "my wiring was severely under code."

One day before Christmas, while sledding on a field near Grandma's, I had gotten snow in my boots and went into her house to dry out. Helping me pull off the wet socks she exclaimed, "Good Lord, child, your feet are cold as ice!"

"Grandma, my feet are like that most of the time." For many years afterwards, she bought me three pair of wool knee socks every Christmas.

BY THE START of first grade, I could walk to the end of our driveway to meet the bus. Mr. Klave patiently stood guard, holding my crutches and offering words of encouragement, as I took a deep breath, grabbed hold of the bus doorway, and heaved myself up the three big steps. This year I would go to school for a full day. I was included in every aspect of school life in one capacity or another. At recess, when the kids jumped rope, I volunteered to be a permanent twirler, and I chanted, "Teddy Bear, Teddy Bear," "Down in the Valley," and "Red Hot Peppers" with the other girls. I rode on teeter-totters, twirled on the merry-go-round, and swung on the swings.

Many times, I rang the bell to signal the end of recess. This was a privilege bestowed upon me by the kindergarten teacher, a young sister who supervised over the noon hour on the playground while the other sisters took their lunch at the convent. Oftentimes, I ended up visiting with her near the end of recess because I could only do so much before I wore out. One day, she surprised me by saying, "Ginger, You're going to be my helper. I'm appointing you as the official bell ringer whenever you want the job." It made me feel important.

VIRGINIA FORD

And then winter arrived. Snow and ice kept me inside if the walkways weren't cleared. On those days, I played board games or card games with Patty, who had asthma and a heart condition.

On December 15, 1952, we got an early Christmas present. Mom gave birth to a nine-pound, healthy baby boy with strawberry blonde hair. He was honored to be given the middle name of Arthur, after my Dad. Jerome Arthur was shortened to Jerry. Everyone said he resembled Daddy more than any of the other boys.

Up to this time, my attendance was perfect. Although I was the only one in my family who came down with polio, I did share measles, chicken pox, and the flu with two of my brothers. I'll never forget the mumps incident in early spring of first grade.

My brother Charlie was missing one afternoon when the bus driver was barreling under the viaduct on the way home from school. I hollered over at Mike, "Where's Charlie?"

He answered nonchalantly, "I don't know. Don't worry about it."

I tried to blink away tears. Where was Charlie? We were supposed to watch out for each other. We were going to be in big trouble.

Sheepishly going into the house, we found Charlie moping on the couch with the left side of his cheek full blown like it was crammed with marshmallows. He looked miserable. Mike laughed like it was the funniest thing he ever saw. The next morning, I was put on the couch with Charlie. My right cheek was swollen to the same size as his left cheek. Mike howled with laughter at us before he caught the bus.

At four o'clock Mike arrived home and was immediately put on the couch with both of his cheeks swollen. He looked like a chipmunk with a mouth full of nuts. Not only was he not laughing, he was mortified. He couldn't stop wiping the tears away. When Dad saw us, he called us "The Three Mumps-Ta-Tears."

NEXT DOOR at Grandma's house, a sensitive incident happened on a summer day, after the end of first grade. It involved my aunt a few months before she married. At this time, she was in her twenties and the delight of my Grandma and Grandpa.

A pretty woman and proud of her Irish heritage, Aunt Alice now reminds me of Scarlett O'Hara. My sisters, Frankie and Donna, always looked up to her in awe. They were excited about being junior bridesmaids in her upcoming wedding.

Mid-morning on a quiet weekday, Grandma and I were sitting at her kitchen table having a pleasant visit when the phone rang. She answered it in the living room on the other side of the house. It must have been an important call. Time passed.

To amuse myself, I picked up a cute ceramic duckling and began a make-believe conversation out loud, like any six-year-old might do. Suddenly a voice growled, "What are you doing in here?" My aunt walked toward me in her slippers, brushing her hair with her ivory-backed hairbrush. I was so startled by her sharp voice and abrupt appearance that the duckling flew out of my hand. Fortunately, I caught it on the edge of the table. Unfortunately, a yellow flower by its webbed foot chipped off.

"Oh, no!" I exclaimed as I fiddled with the chip, trying to it fit into place.

"Now look what you've done." My aunt scrutinized me. "What a pest! A little Miss Busybody. Can't you leave

47

anything alone? Your mother treats you so special. You'll probably grow up to be a spoiled little brat!"

Spoiled? Did she think I was rotten? That I should be thrown out?

"I'm sorry! I didn't mean to drop it. See, it'll be all right. I can glue it back together."

"Oh, no, you don't. I'm not going to let you off the hook in my house!"

This aunt was my godmother. She must have thought that gave her the right to be the boss of me.

Bending over and taking hold of my arms, she shook me fiercely. "Listen, kiddo, I don't care what your mother says, it's about time somebody teaches you a lesson. Just because you have polio, don't think you're going to get away with this. Not while I'm around."

She scowled at me and her dark brows furrowed into the number eleven. I froze, like a wild animal staring into the headlights of oncoming danger. Though frightened, I wasn't about to let her rob me of my mother's love. I stood my ground. I stared her down.

She snatched her hairbrush, pulled me away from the chair and gave me five smart smacks. "Now take that! You're long overdue for a paddling. Somebody's got to do it." When she let me go, I refused to cry. She herded me out the door, dismissing me as "your mother's little pet."

Nonstop tears blinded me as I reached the edge of the sidewalk to the pathway through the orchard. I side-tracked over to a nearby pear tree. I huddled down into the shelter of the tall grass to hide and wiped my face with the ends of my blouse. I gulped big breaths of air and gazed at the clouds overhead. Thanking Jesus that no one had witnessed this humiliation, I wondered why my aunt had been so mean.

The cool breeze and chirping birds soothed my spirit. I found a ripe pear on the ground and bit into it. In time, my head stopped hurting. Sighing with relief, I repeated, "I'm okay, I'm okay." Thinking the incident through, I realized my aunt was right about one thing. I had no memory of ever being spanked. To my knowledge, my sisters had never been spanked, either. I knew I would never forget this one. I learned first-hand the pain a bad temper can inflict. I told myself I'd avoid being alone with her ever again.

Now many decades later, I realize there was some truth in what she had to say about "just because you have polio." Some parents favor their disabled children. And some children use their disability to manipulate others. I remember a pretty girl from the hospital who was the polio poster child for the March of Dimes. The photo showed her standing with crutches and her legs were strapped in metal braces that were attached to Buster Brown shoes. Dressed in a short dress, a bow in her curly hair, she looked like a sweet girl. Her parents were happy to have this image displayed on poster boards, in newspaper ads, and in other public places, but I witnessed times when this girl used her condition to get things she wanted. She'd pull her disability out like a trump card and play on people's sympathy. But I hadn't done that. Hadn't I always tried to be good?

Contrary to what my aunt thought, I've never wanted to be singled out or catered to. I was crushed she felt that way. I decided to keep this incident between Jesus and me and a little girl limped home with a higher level of awareness.

6

LEARNING ABOUT JESUS, LOVING HIM, AND LEANING ON HIM

My SECOND-GRADE YEAR was significant for two reasons—my first surgery and First Eucharist. That year's theme studied in religion classes taught how Jesus loves little children and calls them unto Himself. In September, Father Walsh visited our class to give us a blessing as we prepared for our First Eucharist in the spring. "Jesus is inviting each of you into a more personal relationship with Him. Be open to all He has for you and study hard," he told us. Father had such a love for Jesus and he transmitted that love for Him to me by his heartfelt words and actions. Father Walsh was the first person outside my family to demonstrate how to live the faith. He helped instill in me a lifelong love of Jesus and trust in the Virgin Mary. All fall, I pictured myself sitting at His knee. I sensed the Lord "stoking me up," fortifying me, preparing me.

On the public school bus during the last week of October, all the talk was related to Halloween. The harvest moon cast a warm glow on the clowns, cowboys, and the howling mass of other creatures. Flooding through the gym doors of the village elementary school, we assembled for the ultimate event, the Kiwanis Halloween costume parade and party. In years past, Mike and I were paired as a couple and went trick-or-treating together. Our other brothers and sisters were either too young or too old to participate. Two years earlier, Mike had dressed as Little Boy Blue, and I was Little Bo-Peep. The previous year, he played The Big Bad Wolf and I accompanied him as Little Red Riding Hood. This year, Grandma suggested we dress like a bride and groom.

"That'll be fun," I said. Mike took a lot more convincing. Ultimately, Grandma prevailed. Mom transformed a white sheer curtain panel into a floor-length bridal dress and veil. Donna fashioned my bouquet of yellow chrysanthemums with white ribbon streamers. I felt beautiful.

Mike wore a black suit, white shirt, tie, and a tall black hat made out of a Quaker Oatmeal box. He had a yellow flower in his lapel. Frankie slicked his dark hair back with Brylcreem.

The Halloween march started and the parade began. "Hold tight to my arm. We'll take it real slow," Mike said. Squaring his shoulders, he took my right hand and tucked it into the crook of his arm. That way I wouldn't need my crutches. Taking my first triumphant steps around the gym, we passed the judges' table. Before promenading for the final time, nine-year-old Mike whispered, "I didn't get dressed up in this penguin suit for nothing. Look at the judges and give them a big smile. Remember, we're in it to win it." Mike actually stopped and tipped his hat to them.

Taking the microphone after the music stopped, Mr. Hackney, owner of the local hardware store, announced in a booming voice, "The third place winner is Davy Crockett in the coonskin cap. Second place goes to Dorothy and her little dog Toto. Congratulations!"

By the time he presented them with their awards, my toes tingled and a zing surged through my legs and up my spine, making my heart beat wildly and my face flush. He continued to hold everyone in suspense until he finally shouted, "And the grand prize winners are…the Bride and Groom!"

With a big grin, he winked at me as he shook Mike's hand and presented each of us with a shiny silver dollar.

This success planted the seed of marriage in my young heart confirming that, despite polio, the people who knew me considered me as whole.

Grandma was adamant in deciding to have Mike and I dress up as a bride and groom. Her daughter, my Aunt Alice, got married in the fall and that was all the whole family was thinking and talking about anyway, especially my sisters, Frankie and Donna, who were junior bridesmaids. Grandma would never in a thousand years sway me and steer me toward marriage if she thought it was not in my best interest. In her mind, she wanted to plant marriage in my heart at an early age and to confirm it as a positive possibility. Winning the contest provided additional affirmation as well. Also, I was pleasantly surprised to see how sweetly my Aunt Alice treated me after her marriage.

MIDWAY THROUGH JANUARY, I returned to the hospital for my first surgery and a two-week-stay. This time, I was old enough to understand a little bit more about what was happening to me.

In technical terms, my medical record states: *Lambrinudi's type of triple arthodesis of the left foot. Tenodesis of thetibialis anticus and the peroneal longus left. And foot placed in a long cast.* That means my surgeon performed a triple fusion, using three screws in my left ankle and mid-foot. He also lengthened two tendons to better balance my foot so the fusion would not have an abnormal pull on it due to the muscle imbalance and anomaly of my left foot, which was turning outward.

I remember having to fast from food and drink the night before the surgery. I hated the red sign that was posted on the room door that ordered "nothing by mouth." I was so thirsty my mouth felt like sandpaper.

I became distracted when a spooky older woman visited. No one told me she was coming. Dressed in a yellow uniform, with her hair pulled into a bun and confined under a brown hairnet, she said gloomily, "I'm here to prep you." I didn't have a clue what that meant. She uncovered scary-looking equipment and proceeded to shave my leg and wash the areas to be operated on with a special soap called Phisoderm.

This strange woman scared me speechless. It was frightening to have her use a straight razor on me like those used in old western movies. When she finished, she abruptly packed up her cart, towels and tools, turned off the light, and silently departed.

But that wasn't the last scary occurrence. I had another unexpected visitor—a young man in a rumpled short white coat who said, "I'm here to draw blood." I was convinced he'd bleed me dry. After he filled two big vials of blood, it took me a long time to go to sleep. I was afraid to think of who might come through the door next.

Jesus listened to my woes and gave me His peace and strength. I lay in bed thinking about how thirsty Jesus was when he hung on the cross and I tried to offer my pre-surgery fast for the poor souls in purgatory. In time, I slept poorly, tossing and turning and worrying most of the night, wondering what would be in store for me. Finally, the day dawned.

With cracked lips and my mouth feeling like it was full of dry cotton, I was strapped onto a stretcher, and a nurse gave me an injection to make me "woozy." My roommates wished me good luck. Mom pinned a *My Mother, My Confidence* scapular to the top of my gown while whispering a prayer. Kissing me, she said "I'm going to go to the hospital chapel and pray for you. I'll be right here when you come back."

My old friend Tony whisked me away. An IV was inserted into my arm and a rubber mask was put over my nose and mouth. I was told to breathe deeply. Within seconds, the ether took effect. The bright overhead ceiling lights spun. A blissful darkness ensued.

I woke up in a gray fog aching with excruciating pain, nauseated, and intensely thirsty. The nurse offered a teaspoon of ice chips for me to suck. Mom swam into my view. She called me a brave girl as she inspected me all over. She wiped my face with a warm cloth and doled out small amounts of ice, promising if I kept them down, I could have sips of Vernor's ginger ale.

The next two weeks, my nurses used me like a pincushion, poking me with penicillin shots to reduce the risk of infection and giving me pain shots every four hours. At one time, my bottom was so black and blue from shots, the nurse said she didn't know where to put the next injection. My blood-stained cast was propped on pillows to ease the swelling and bleeding. If someone bumped into the bed, I howled.

I was usually a pretty easygoing and happy kid, but post-op time was no joke. I was consumed by more kinds of pain than I could count and incessant itching under my full-length cast. I became adept at finding things to scratch with to provide some relief. Rulers, knitting needles, even the stainless steel dinner knife that I stashed away in the drawer of my bedstand worked to scratch with.

My second-grade classmates were used to my comings and goings for medical appointments. They sent me cards, jokes, and pictures which my nurse hung up. It made me feel connected to the real world.

To bear the burden of the long hours and days of stifling confinement to a bed, my roommates and I tried to amuse ourselves by playing "I Spy" and other easy games we made up. "From A to Z, I'm As Thankful As Can Be" was our favorite because it made us think of happy things. The rules were simple—say each letter of the alphabet one at a time and then recite the first things that come to your mind that you are thankful for. I remember a few of my choices. "A - Apples, B - Bubble Bath, C - Chocolate Chip Cookies, D - Dolls, E - Easter Egg Hunt, F - Felix the Cat, G - Gumballs, H - Hummingbird." Though not too exciting, it helped heal our spirits. We desperately waited for better times and better places.

At last the day arrived when I could go home. In our tiny bedroom with the cowboy (no cowgirl) wallpaper, I was pleasantly surprised to find the bigger bed replaced with two single cots on either side of the room. Mom said, "I didn't want your brothers jarring your casted leg. One of the beds is for you and the other is for Charlie and Dominic. Take your pick. Mike has moved downstairs with Bob."

In February, I was back in school and my religion classes continued to bolster my spirit and enrich my faith. In my heart, I knew the torturous first surgery had tightened the bond between me and Jesus. It gave me some inkling of what He suffered during His crucifixion. The nuns and priest did an excellent job helping me prepare my soul. In May, I was ready to receive Jesus in the Eucharist.

This tomboy had to dress appropriately. Being raised with seven brothers, I could get down and dirty. Mom's big job was to make a six-month-old, dingy-looking cast respectable. She sat me on the counter top in the kitchen and scrubbed it with Ajax so it would look decent against my white communion dress and veil and eventually succeeded in making it dazzle. She put my hair in banana curls. Finally, I passed muster.

The first communion class began this special event by solemnly proceeding down the aisle. Glowing candles and lilies made an impressive walkway. When it was time, my classmates walked up the steps in single file to receive the host at the main altar. Because I couldn't climb the steps with my cast and crutches, I waited at the communion rail.

Father Walsh brought the sacred host down to me. Joy and peace filled my heart as I embraced Jesus as my personal savior at this early age. I promised to receive the Holy Eucharist often and welcomed Jesus to be in the middle of my life—centering me. I know that living in this worrisome world, He will continue to help me through my difficulties, no matter how big or small. When feelings of isolation grab hold of me, I know I am not alone. Jesus accompanies me on my journey, now and forever.

The following week, my class presented an after-school program of poems, songs and skits to honor our earthly mothers and our heavenly Mother, Mary. Sister Therese Marie assigned me a poem to present. When the curtain parted, I stood in a walking cast and crutches, wearing a pastel blue dress, next to a large statue of Mary surrounded with bouquets of garden flowers. I recited Mary Dixon Thayer's poem, "Lovely Lady Dressed in Blue," which is about Mary's relationship with her son, Jesus.

Many times, this poem became my consolation. It made me realize that prayer is simply talking to Jesus. I can do it any time and in any place. And I had plenty of time to talk to Jesus.

X-RAYS SHOWED my bones were not entirely healed, so I was disappointed to learn that the cast would not come off in time for the end-of-the-year festivities. Our school picnic was held in June. There is a picture of me in a dress looking disgruntled, standing with crutches next to kids in swimsuits.

I had hoped to shock my classmates by showing them how I could swim out to the big dock and dive into the drop-off. I dreamed about how they'd be so surprised to see me swim like a fish. This would be the one and only chance for me to outshine the best of them. Instead, beached on the sidelines in the scorching heat, I sulked while everyone else splashed and laughed and cooled down in the spring-fed lake. Sure enough, none of my classmates went into the water deeper than their waist. Though angry and disappointed, I worked hard to conceal my disappointment when they all came back on land to eat. It would have been so great to do something none of them could do. Instead, I had to swallow my pride, and I wondered for the hundredth time why I caught polio, when none of my friends, or even my siblings did.

SOON AFTER THE PICNIC, another x-ray proved the bone had healed. As I sat on the exam table, the putrid yellow walls of the tiny cast room matched my feelings of doom and gloom. I was glad to be getting it off, but I was scared of the procedure. "Are you ready?" the doctor asked. I didn't have a choice. He quickly slipped his protective goggles over his eyes and started the saw. The noise sounded like a gigantic, whining mosquito and sent shivers up and down my spine. Each time the blade bore down into the hard plaster, dust and bits of plaster chips spit everywhere. I was frightened that I'd be cut with the mean-looking blade. My teeth chattered uncontrollably.

The doctor pried the cast open with big tongs and threw

57

the stinky thing into a large waste container. Then he cut
and peeled the cotton wrap. The smell of my exposed leg
was obnoxious. I thought my shriveled limb looked
repulsive, but, the procedure wasn't over yet. The doctor
removed my stitches one by one with a snip of scissors and
a tug of the tweezers. I yelped at each pull-out and started
to cry. I couldn't help it when I saw blood. The doctor
finally finished, telling me the incision had healed nicely
and praising my courage.

The trip home was unusually difficult. The slightest
jarring caused excruciating pain because my knee was
frozen. It hadn't bent for six months. Those first few days at
home found me constantly guarding my leg from being
bumped. I felt like a turtle without its shell. The scars left in
my skin after the stitches were removed hurt. The scars on
my ankles and feet were—and still are—sensitive and
painful if they are banged or hit. They burn searingly,
bringing tears to my eyes. The sensation was—and still is—
bad. I had to hold my breath until it subsided.

I started physical therapy to get the knee to bend and it
was pure torture. Bending the knee little by little in warm
water bath soaks, and later in the pool or lake, offered the
most benefit in getting it to be flexible. It took a good two
months for my knee to begin to bend normally.

I HAD great role models while growing up. Mom's love of
the faith was ingrained in me at a tender age. I am the
product of her influence, teaching, and training. As her
namesake, I strove to emulate her. The best part of me came
from her. During the long, lonely days in the hospital, I took
ownership of the faith due primarily to Mom's fine
example. She was my mainstay. Scripture passages, family
prayers, and the hymns I memorized saved me many times

over from sinking into despair when I was separated from her. They brought me comfort and hope.

My grandparents taught me to be a prayer warrior. For years, they attended the Sorrowful Mother Novena on Friday evenings in Pinckney. This novena petitions Mary, the mother of Jesus, to intercede before the throne of God on our behalf. Since First Eucharist in May, I knew I truly loved Jesus and I realized that spending time with Him was a privilege. The backseat of my grandparents' VW Bug had room, so they always invited Mom and me to attend. We were delighted to accept. We sang and worshipped together during this special devotion.

In God's house, I found peace. The old St. Mary's Church had beautiful altars. Two life-sized statues of angels, kneeling in adoration with their heads bowed, were on either side of the main altar. Their humble posture and devotion awed me. The service always ended with the song "Goodnight, Sweet Jesus, Goodnight." I grew to love this song. I sang it softly at bedtime. The lyrics freed me from any bad thoughts or fears, reassuring me that Jesus stood guard watching over me.

Our family prayed the daily rosary and meditated on the Joyful Mysteries on Monday and Thursday, the Sorrowful Mysteries on Tuesday and Friday, and the Glorious Mysteries on Wednesday, Saturday, and Sunday. These prayers reflect on the history of salvation, from the annunciation of the birth of Jesus to the coronation of His mother. After studying the life of Jesus all school year, the themes of the rosary became more meaningful to me this particular summer. By God's grace, I was growing in greater appreciation for my faith. Next to holy mass, the rosary kept us united in our faith.

During this summer, incidental things also left their mark on me. Grandpa worked at the post office all day and Grandma was home alone next door. Since my only playmates were Mike, Charlie and Dominic, I took a lot of comfort in visiting at Grandma's, especially since my Aunt Alice was married and out of the house. Also, Mom was heavily pregnant with another baby and she took a long nap with little Jerry during the hot afternoons.

On the occasions Grandma permitted me to go upstairs in her house to play, she'd call out in a loud, emphatic voice, "Be sure and close the doors behind you!" She was afraid of mice. They were occasionally caught in a trap in that old storage room.

The clock on the fireplace mantle chimed out the hour, and I softly sang the lyrics Grandma taught me to the melody of the Westminster Chimes. "Lord through this hour, be Thou our guide, so by Thy power, no foot shall slide."

Most people would think of sliding into sin. However, my prayer petitioned that I literally not slide to the floor. I'd softly sing this little refrain to myself inside and outside of Grandma's house.

The garments hanging from the clothes hook on the back side of the door swished as I opened the door to the stairway, quickly scooted in, and closed it tightly. Beyond this door, I found three childhood treasures whose messages are a part of my religious fabric. I climbed the first twelve stairs, one at a time, straight up the narrow passageway to the landing where I would pause and catch my breath. A chandelier hung from the ceiling. A large double-pane window let in a flood of light. Next to the window was my first treasure, a nineteenth-century picture of a frail elderly lady with a puckered face. Resting in a high-back chair, she gazed outward with a smile. She was wearing a black dress with a white collar and a ruffled cap on her head. A healthy girl, around the age of five, sat on the arm of the chair, entwining her arms around the woman. Her smile was radiant and full of love.

I really liked this picture. I identified with the girl and her great love and respect for her grandmother. I was blessed with elders to cherish and with whom I share special bonds. The promise underneath the picture says, "I'll Take Care of You." This promise was echoed in my family throughout my childhood. Every day, Mom sent us out the door, saying, "Watch out for each other." Dad often assured Mom, "Don't worry, I'll see to it." Grandma often said, "Take care of yourself. Watch your step. You're special to me," when I headed home.

The second treasure was a picture of a teenage girl with black hair flowing down the back of her blue nightgown as she knelt at the side of her bed. Underneath the picture is a prayer of childhood I still cherish. "God, grant me this precious grace. Make my heart Thy dwelling place. Let us live together hence. You and I and innocence."

My third treasure was the spare bedroom and the storehouse for family memorabilia. This was the perfect sanctuary to dream and wonder about relatives and relics from the past. I found World War II letters and postcards from my godfather, Uncle Bill, prom dresses, costume jewelry, and a wealth of other treasures. Grandma allowed me to explore this room when the weather was cold, snowy, or rainy. When I returned to the kitchen, Grandma would ask, "What do you do up there?" Little by little, I learned to put events and names and faces to the family tree, helping me understand and appreciate my heritage.

During the latter years of the Great Depression my parents were given a parcel of my grandparent's farmland as a wedding gift. The property is located in the countryside two miles north of the village of Dexter, sandwiched in with Wylie road in the far back of the land and fronted by Dexter-Pinckney Road at the end of the driveway by a tall oak tree.

My parents thought it would be a great place to raise a

family. It was a land rich with deer, turkeys, and pheasants for hunting, berries and apples for preserves, nuts for baking, and a nearby lake which would provide plenty of fresh water fish for Friday fish-fries. Here they constructed a two-story modest home to the best of their ability.

Three unheated bedrooms were upstairs. The downstairs consisted of a kitchen, bathroom, and a bigger family room with a large table and benches for dining and captain chairs at either end where my Mom and Dad presided at mealtimes. The rest of the room held a couch, a rocking chair and two stuffed chairs. A large braided rug covered the main floor. A Kalamazoo wood and coal burning stove took up one corner and a three-cornered cupboard holding dinnerware stood from floor to ceiling in another. The walls were covered in knotty pine and on the east and south walls windows with homemade curtains let in a cheery light. To gain access to the front of the house you'd climb up four cement steps to the stoop. The kitchen door led to the back porch and yard.

A Michigan basement, which meant it had a dirt floor, was under a portion of the house. It served my Dad with a work table in the center of the room with an overhead light and it held shelving on the back-wall for canned goods from the large garden my parents cultivated just beyond the back yard, chicken coop and coal shed.

I was one of the first Baby Boomers to be born in April of 1946 and the sixth Visel child. When I turned six we had more than a full house. Some of my older siblings were very close to going out into the world while three younger siblings were under me. During this time, an addition was made to our house, adding two more bedrooms and a large living room with a fieldstone fireplace. The outside of both the old and new parts of the house was covered over with white aluminum siding and black shingles and trim. A new front door entered into the new living room. The old front stoop and door were removed. Shrubbery and flowers were added under the front windows and the front driveway was turned into a circular driveway with additional parking space for the older set of children, who one by one acquired cars of their own.

My parents never required any older children to pay room or board. However, the kids helped out in various ways when they could. My older brothers helped do a lot of the construction work with our Dad. Both my older sisters took it upon themselves to furnish the new living room. They paid to have it carpeted and bought a matching couch and chair set, a coffee table, end tables, and two lamps and new material for curtains. They also wanted to have this more formal "normal" room to receive their dates.

Donna and Frankie also claimed one of the bedrooms and paid for everything. They put in turquoise wall paint and carpeting, bunk beds with white chenille bedspreads, a decorative milk-white ceiling light, a large dresser with mirror and a chest and a white telephone and a record player. Plus, they paid to have a lock with their own set of keys installed in their door. By this time in their late teens they deserved a little privacy. Bob and Mike had the other bedroom with bunk beds, a full closet and a dresser.

We were an energetic, rowdy, and loud group, but we survived and have shared the common threads that bound us all together.

On August 15, 1954, a joyous event occurred. Ann Theresa was born. She was Visel child number ten. Finally, a sister! I was distanced by a seven and eight-year age span from my two older sisters, who were very close. With three older brothers and three younger brothers, this baby sister was a pleasant surprise. Ann was like a living, breathing doll I helped feed, bathe, and dress.

IN THE LATE afternoon on a dismal January day in 1955, my right leg was set in a plaster cast and strung up in traction. It persistently throbbed in pain from my second surgery, which had been performed three days earlier. My left arm was sore and bruised from the IV tube that had been removed. I felt like a wounded animal caught in a trap.

My medical records for this surgery read: *Right triple arthrodesis. A well-padded short-leg cast was applied. The cast was split longitudinally to allow for future swelling.* Translated, this means that a triple fusion on my right ankle and mid-foot was performed. These fusions were to stabilize my ankle and mid-foot to prevent collapse of my mid-foot and arch area as well as prevent foot drop.

When Mom arrived, she told me about an upsetting incident on the day of my surgery. On that morning, she drove my brother Dick's old green Ford and parked in the lot on the side of the hospital. The car was stolen. It was recovered two days later, abandoned, with an empty gas tank, sixty miles away. Thankfully, there was no further damage.

Shortly afterwards, the day brightened. The nurse liltingly announced, "You've got mail." To my delight, she reached into her pocket and handed me not one, but two pieces of mail—a postcard and a letter.

"This has got to be a mistake," I said disappointed. "I don't know anyone in Oahu." I inspected the postcard showing a Polynesian man in a colorful shirt picking a pineapple off a spiky three-foot plant.

"No, that's your name," said the nurse.

Turning the card over, I realized it was from my brother Dick. *Hi Sis, Aloha! I've joined the Navy for a two-year stint. My ship is named the U.S.S. Yorktown. This baby is big with a flight deck for aircraft carriers and helicopters. We are in port on the island of Oahu and ship out in two days. Today I swam in the Pacific Ocean! Hope your surgery went well. Sharpen your*

pencil, I expect you to write me. I'll send an address soon.
Love, Dick

The nurse laughed. "Good, I can see it made you feel better."

Before she left, I asked, "Where's Oahu?"

"Get your geography book out and find it on the map. Here's a hint. Look below the coast of California and find the Hawaiian Islands."

With so many children at home and keeping track of their various activities, Mom never mentioned a word about Dick being in the Navy. What else was I missing while I was away from home? I shut my eyes and dreamed about sitting on a warm sandy beach, listening to the soothing ocean surf under a palm tree while sucking on juicy pineapple. When I woke from my nap, I read Dick's news again. His mail opened my eyes to the world and was the beginning of my desire to travel and experience new places, especially Hawaii.

In the following week, I read everything I could find on Hawaii and pineapples. I sent away to the Dole Pineapple Company for their free recipe booklet. Then, a small package arrived from Oahu. Dick had sent me a Hawaiian doll! It was going to be great fun tracking my big brother on his adventures in the Pacific.

One particular afternoon began to drag once my "blah" lunch was picked over. I was bored, really bored. A tiny spider caught my attention. I monitored its moves from one corner to another, and then amazingly, to all four corners.

From start to finish, it traveled the ceiling in twenty-five minutes. My thoughts were interrupted by a curly blonde from the Galen Society, who chimed merrily, "Mail for a Miss Ginger Visel." She handed me the envelope with a big smile. Glancing at the return address, I exclaimed, "It's from my Aunt Pearl!" A crisp dollar bill dropped into my

lap when I opened the card and read her cheery "get well."
Oh boy, a windfall!

I perked up, feeling daring, I hatched an idea to escape
for a while when I saw the wheelchair at the head of my
bed. If Dick could go to Hawaii, I could go to the gift
shop. Clutching my money, I carefully slipped into the
chair, put a pillow on the outstretched leg extension, and
propped my casted leg on it. Taking a deep breath and
looking both ways before exiting the doorway, I
cautiously rolled out of the room, breezed past the
nursing station and the nurse talking on the telephone
with her back to me, slid by patient rooms, past the utility
room to the end of the hall, and out to the elevators.
Ta-dah!

I had never before left the floor unescorted. I'd never
even thought about doing it. I felt free. Mom always said,
"God helps those who help themselves." I figured if an itsy-
bitsy spider could make it all the way around my room in a
short time, I could succeed in this little adventure. Thus
inspired, I continued on my mission. I wanted to find
something tasty after that disappointing lunch. I exited the
elevator at the main floor.

While making a beeline to the hospital store, all I could
think of was a popular advertisement on the black-and-
white television. A giraffe said in a deep voice, "I want a
Clark Bar!" I figured it would be the best medicine for me
right now, even if the doctor didn't order it.

Spying the bright orange wrapper with big blue letters
in the candy section, I chose two nickel bars. Then, from the
gum section, I added three five-stick packages, which were
also five cents each.

I paid the clerk and dumped the change into the small
brown bag with the wrapped treats, which I quickly stashed
under my hospital gown. I wheeled myself onto the
elevator and re-traced my route to my floor with no one the

wiser. From start to finish, I calculated my time by the hall clock—twenty-five minutes.

Safely back in bed, I peeled the wrapper off the candy bar and took a mouthful of the sweet chocolate, savoring it as it slowly melted on my tongue. Mission accomplished. I got a Clark Bar!

In that moment, I felt great, like the rich and the famous, as I luxuriated in my achievement and reaped the reward of my pursuit. Even though my only audience was the spider in the corner, I felt triumphant as I gave him a thumbs-up and took another bite of my candy bar.

Days later, back at home, it didn't take me long to make a pineapple-upside-down cake with Mom's help and Dick's inspiration. The kitchen was off-limits to me when major meals were being prepared, since we cooked for such a large family. Mom decided that having me near heavy iron skillets and hot kettles of soup wasn't safe. But when the kitchen wasn't too busy, I sat at a side-counter cutting out cookies or making a cake. I resolved to make my brother Dick a pineapple-upside-down cake when he finished his service days.

OUR LETTERS CONTINUED BACK and forth over the Pacific. Dick was proud of his ship, his shipmates, and daily life. In addition to his regular responsibilities, he did clerical work in the chaplain's office and served at daily Mass. Occasionally he sent photographs in his letters—pictures of planes landing on the flight deck, the mess hall, and tablemates, Dick sitting at the typewriter in the office, the ship's exterior when in port, Japanese children, works of art, and all the sailors lined up. He asked me questions about school and life at home.

My letters reported on the weather, our activities, and

family news. I told him when a younger sibling lost a baby tooth, who shot a deer, who caught a mess of fish, or the latest adventures with Blackie the dog.

From far, far, away during his tour of duty with the US Navy, Dick became a mentor for my studies in geography, writing, and spelling. He wrote, "Ginger girl, keep those letters coming. You tell me more news from the home front than anyone else." He was starved for news from home, just like I was when I was hospitalized.

His letters encouraged me to work harder in school and get good grades. Dick praised me if Mom wrote him and told him I had won a weekly spelling bee or if I used descriptive words and "big girl" vocabulary. I told him how Mom chose words from the vocabulary page in the *Reader's Digest* and challenged us to spell them correctly and use them correctly in our writing and conversation. In fact, Dick is credited with being the first one to predict that I would become a writer. And, thanks to him, my geography grades soared.

When he finished his tour of duty, Dick gave me one of his retired sailor hats as a souvenir. It was my favorite hat to wear when I went boating until it finally wore out. He also gave his high school sweetheart, Shirley, a diamond ring. Soon after, they were married. For this wedding, I got to shop for a new outfit with Mom at Goodyear's Department Store. I had no trouble choosing the perfect dress—a navy blue sailor dress with a red tie.

7

THE MONKEY IN THE MIDDLE

SEVERAL X-RAYS WERE a standard part of my regular three-month outpatient check-up visits. They involved my laying down on the x-ray table without a pillow for pictures of my spine and hips. This was followed with images shot of my legs and feet. Oftentimes, sandbags were used for different positioning.

I was growing fast, and doctors were concerned about my rapid growth spurts. Their focus was on the curvature of my spine. What could the medical world do to curtail further damage as I grew in height, other than perform a spinal fusion? Dr. Badgley, along with my mother, had agreed to try to avoid a procedure that severe if at all possible. So far, physical therapy and routine swimming were successful, but would they continue to avert more of a curve? Now, a different type of x-ray was introduced for this study.

Clothed in a hospital gown, I followed the technician into the claustrophobic x-ray room. The solid door closed behind me with a loud thud as my heart resonated with the same sound. A sense of trepidation overwhelmed me, and I

VIRGINIA FORD

breathed deeply in an effort to fight the suffocating feeling.
Instead of using the step stool to climb onto the x-ray table,
the technician directed me to do something different.
"Please stand in front of the white panel on the wall." He
positioned my feet on the painted footprints below me and
straightened my shoulders while pressing them backwards
until they touched the panel. Placing his finger under my
chin he tilted my head upward, saying, "Look forward.
Stand as straight and tall as you can. Lightly hold onto the
grab bars on either side of you to steady yourself."

In the past, Mom had questioned the excessive numbers
of x-rays needed, concerned about my exposure to so much
radiation, but nothing changed. The x-rays continued to be
required. But until now, nothing was freaky. But now, the
technician took the end of a rope that threaded through a
pulley, released it and down dropped a headgear made of
leather straps in the shape of a football helmet. He fit the
jerry-rigged gizmo over my head, fastening it with a
padded chin-strap that buckled on the side of my right jaw.
When I looked aghast, he explained, "Your doctors want x-
rays of your back in a stretched-out position. Don't be
afraid. This will be uncomfortable, but it won't hurt you."

Slowly he stretched me. He literally strung me up while
ordering me to let go of the grab bars. Once I was on my
tip-toes, he wound the rope around a cleat to secure it.
Quickly he went in the cubby and fiddled with a machine.

I could only muster an "M-mmm, M-mmm" through
my clamped lips to his ridiculous question, "Are you
okay?" Tears dribbled down my cheeks. I surrendered
helplessly to this treatment which must have made me look
like a dead deer hoisted on a buck pole.

After the x-ray was taken, the technician kept me
dangling for two repeats as he changed the film. This was a
difficult experience. It wounded me physically, but
especially emotionally, making me feel like a battered piece

70

of meat. By the time this ordeal had ended, I worried that all my blood had drained to my feet. They felt as heavy as cement. My knees were painfully strained. My hips felt like they had popped out of their sockets. I was afraid my neck was as long as a giraffe's, because I must have been at least a foot taller by then.

The first thing I did when I was released from the torture chamber and my circulation returned to normal was to find a bathroom with a mirror to check myself for drastic changes, especially my neck. I guessed that the procedure was a test to see if any new corrective appliance might help. Sure enough, shortly after consulting with the doctors, an appointment was scheduled for me at the Appliance Shop.

The back brace man, Mr. Nordman, was tall with caterpillar eyebrows and black hair. He had a hacky cough and smelled like cigarettes. He worked in the hot shop with only fans providing ventilation, and he had large sweat rings under his arms, staining his shirt. His personality made up for these imperfections. I thought he must be a great father to his children. He was jolly, gentle, and tried his best to make the appliance comfortable. "If I do my job right, this will help correct your posture and, we hope, prevent more curvature of your spine."

I abhorred this back brace. Two sturdy metal bars ran down my back and two ran under my arms to my waist. They were covered in leather and attached to a top and bottom circular frame that fit around my middle. It was put on like a saddle, cinched over my chest and stomach with straps to hold it in place. A crutch-like top was fastened to the brace under my right arm to raise my droopy shoulder. It turned me into a marionette, stiff and upright. I could only bend from the waist. Mr. Nordman called it a pelvic girdle, but I said, "It sure doesn't look like any girdle my Grandma and Mom wear."

Although Mr. Nordman did his best to make the device

form-fitting and padded for comfort, it was barely tolerable. I had to coat my torso with baby powder and wear an undershirt to keep it from sticking to me. This device became a part of me for eight hours every day for two years.

Some of the girls in my class bragged about getting training bras. They couldn't imagine what was under my clothes.

BROTHERS AND SISTERS can become either the bane or blessing of a child's existence. Mine were both. When Ann was a little over a year old, she shared the bed with me. I called her my "little snuggle bunny." The boys' cowboy wallpaper was replaced with a pink floral design on a baby blue background. The final touch that made this the girls' room was when Dad installed two shelves to hold my doll collection.

Mike, age nine, let me know how he felt about the loss of his old bedroom. He found it amusing to switch the heads and limbs of my dolls and to mix them up every which way when no one was around to catch him in the act.

Mike, who was the youngest until I was born, was more aware of the extra attention paid to me than the others. He didn't go around making a mission of causing grief to anyone except me. I imagine Mike regarded polio as something that was attention-getting for me and unfair treatment for him. I can still hear him say, "How come she gets another glass of chocolate milk?" My parents were always encouraging me to eat foods that had lots of calcium to heal and strengthen my bones. He was also irritated to hear Grandma refer to me as "My Dolly." He felt slighted, and, he pinched me whenever he heard her call me by this endearment.

One summer night he hatched a plan to put a few big juicy nightcrawlers between the flowered print sheets in our bed. I could tell he was up to something. After surveying our room and finding nothing out of order, I pulled back the bedcovers. Sure enough, there was the evidence. However, during their day's hiatus in the bed, the worms had become shriveled and dried out. Mike didn't get much satisfaction out of this antic because I didn't scream— after all, I liked to fish. I told Mike that he was disgusting. Dad gave him a spanking.

Mike's pranks evolved as he grew, but they never topped the day with the snake. He and another boy down the road liked to catch and play with snakes. This particular day, Mike brought a big garter snake into the kitchen, where I was doing dishes. "Leave me be! Take it outside!" I ordered. Instead, Mike laughed and dropped it on the floor. It started to slide along the baseboard. I hopped up on the kitchen stool and screamed. Outside in the garden, Mom and Dad heard my shriek. They hurried inside. Snakes were my nemesis because I couldn't run away from them. "Take that snake out behind the woodpile and let it go. Then wait there for me," Dad ordered. Mike not only got a lecture about growing up, but a sound licking as well.

Several months went by without any pranks or derogatory remarks from Mike. And then winter weather arrived. We slept upstairs in unheated bedrooms. On frigid nights Mom or Dad would drape a flannel sheet on the Kalamazoo stove to warm it up and holler, "Tell me when you're in bed," while I climbed the stairs. Once I was settled, one of them would tuck the sheet with its enveloping warmth all around me, especially my freezing cold feet, and pile other blankets on top before tramping downstairs. Mike whispered from his room, "Nighty night, you big baby."

His nasty pranks and verbal put-downs actually did me

a favor. Mike helped to toughen my hide and helped me become less emotionally fragile—a trait that would stand me in good stead in the future.

In spite of all the ways he found to harass me, I'll always be grateful for the many good deeds Mike performed during these early years. He was helpful when we had to cross the street in front of the bus. If the driveway turned into a slippery slope, he offered me his strong arm and helped me struggle home without me asking. During winter play times, he pulled me to the pond on the toboggan. When it was time to go home, he grabbed the rope after I was safely on board and plowed through the snow. The same was true when we went sledding on the big hill in the cow field. We flew down the hill and afterwards he would chug back up the hill, pulling me on the toboggan. He was a hardy, strong boy. When I thanked him, he told me gruffly, "That's okay. You're a lightweight."

Mike's childhood behavior reminds me of a little girl described in a Mother Goose nursery rhyme. "When she was good, she was very, very good, and when she was bad, she was horrid."

Late in the afternoon on a frigid Friday when I was in fifth grade, the students were in church for a Lenten Service called The Stations of the Cross. After services ended, we were pelted with hailstones and freezing rain. The steps became treacherous and the sidewalk leading back to the school was coated with ice. Everyone hurried to the safety of the waiting buses. I lingered in the shadows of the vestibule as the others stormed past me.

Luckily for me, Mike, who served as an altar boy, had stayed back to snuff candles and remove his surplice. He was on his way out when he saw me. "What in the heck are you doing standing in the darkened entranceway?" he asked. After I explained my predicament, he grabbed his buddy and said, "Help me make a chair seat." They put

74

their hands together and I gratefully hopped aboard, putting my arms around their broad shoulders. I hung on tight as they carried me to the bus, making it a game to show how strong and clever they were. When Mike was good, he was very, very good.

"IT'S A BOY!" my Dad announced proudly as he came into the house mid-morning on August 15, 1956, the year I turned ten. He headed for the refrigerator and poured himself a glass of iced tea. Those who were home gathered around him as Dad sat at the table. "Your new brother is as cute as a button. He and your mother are doing fine. She's got this next week to rest in bed to get her strength back. And she has a wonderful nurse taking good care of her. She sends her love to you all."

I hopped up on Dad's knee, "What did you name the baby?"

"Paul Thaddeus." Giving my ponytail a tug, he chuckled, "He's the caboose. I guess that makes you the monkey in the middle. With five older and five younger siblings, you have a pretty special place."

I was ten when Paul was born. Above me were Dick, Frankie, Donna, Bob and Mike. Below me were Charlie, Dominic, Jerry, Ann and Paul. Eleven children in twenty-one years. No wonder Mom and Dad were done!

The middle child has a unique perspective on the family dynamics. I knew the worlds of both the older children and the younger ones. I guess what Dad called me was true. I did play the role of the monkey in the middle. I often saw myself catching little life lessons from the older ones and passing them on to the younger ones.

I missed Mom. But it was good that she got a break. It was not easy taking care of a newborn. But by raising a big family she was earning her wings. When she came home with the baby in her arms, she said, "Now I can say, *To Heaven with Eleven*."

Visions of her in our kitchen, holding a baby on her hip with one hand while stirring a pot of stew with the other came to mind. Her hands kneaded dough into bread or rolled it out to cut biscuits on Saturdays and prepared delicious meals day after day. Every spring, summer, and fall she planted, weeded and harvested, canned, froze, and made preserves for the long winter ahead. Skilled at sewing, her hands turned fabric into clothing and pajamas for all her children. Then there was the tiresome task of laundry day—sorting clothes, washing them in a wringer washer, hanging them out to dry, and ironing them. It took years before my parents could afford to install a Maytag washer and dryer.

I remember Mom knitting dozens of scarves, mittens, hats, socks and slippers in cheery colors and patterns. She bathed us, making it fun with, "Rub-a-dub-dub, three men in a tub" ditties and songs. Her hands flipped the pages of our bedtime stories and lovingly tucked us into bed, folding our hands into prayer as she prayed over us. Her hands cared for us night and day if we were sick with a fever or flu, chicken pox, colds, mumps, measles—and, polio too.

For years, it was her hands that massaged my back and paralyzed legs and faithfully put me through rigorous physical therapy. She taught me to swim and to love the water, the best exercise of all. For three summers, she rowed the boat over and back across the lake as I swam alongside it for daily exercise.

I remember the time I was feeling blue and she stopped stirring the soup, turned it down, took my hands in hers and started twirling me around the kitchen singing, "Dance Little Dollie with a hole in your stockin' and your knees keep a knockin' and your toes keep a rockin', dance Little

76

Dollie with a hole in your stockin' dance by the light of the moon." She had her own special way of making me laugh and cheering me up. Most important of all, she taught us our faith by living it and praying the family rosary with us every evening in our living room, on her knees with her beads in her hands.

Life would be easier for us when Mom came home, and harder for her. She did so much for every one of us. I wished I could do special things for her. I wished I could make her breakfast and carry it upstairs and serve it to her in bed. On laundry day, I would like to be able to hang the wash outside on the clothesline during the warm weather. I would like to hike down near the river like Mike and gather spring pussy willows that she loved to put in a vase and place on the kitchen windowsill to admire. It would be great if I could cook her a fabulous meal. Maybe someday I'd be able to do these things and more.

Frankie knew that she wanted to become an early-elementary teacher from her first day of college. She started me thinking about my future. After graduating from Eastern Michigan University, Frankie lived at home for two years while she taught second grade in our local public school. I loved hearing about her students' challenges and successes. Frankie allowed me to play teacher by checking math and spelling papers. She gave me practice papers and books to teach our youngest brothers and sister to read and write.

Charlie and Dominic were in scouting, with Mom as the den mother. That meant all meetings were held at our house. I was Mom's helper for the craft projects. I enjoyed tutoring and assisting and grew into the idea of teaching as I tried to emulate Frankie. I felt as though I was practicing for what might come later, and I pointed my personal compass in that direction.

WHEN I WAS ten years old, during November of 1956, I was hospitalized for my third and fourth surgeries. They were the most memorable surgeries of my childhood. My medical records read: *November 1956: Combined release of originis of tenso femoris, Sartorius, and rectus femoris, plus release of Bigelow's ligament about the left hip and release of the iliotibial band just proximal to the knee. Patient was placed in a spica cast with the right leg in adduction and the left leg in full extension and adduction.*

Translated to ordinary terms, my third surgery was to release (cut) the muscles and tendons about my left hip as I was developing a hip flexion contracture which would have prevented me from standing straight. My pelvis and leg were cast in a fully extended position to gain as much range of motion as possible while my surgical areas were healing.

Two weeks later, *November 1956: Suter-Yount fasciotomy, right lower extremity. Patient was casted with both hips in full extension and the legs adducted as much as possible.* This fourth surgery was to release the tissue around my right hip, to prevent me from developing a hip contracture.

Just before the ether took full effect for this fourth surgery, the doctor, asked "What's your favorite color?"

"Blue."

Upon awakening, I found myself in a bright turquoise body cast. I looked and felt like a beached baby whale— blue and totally incapacitated! No one had so much as hinted that I'd be in a body cast. I cried an ocean of tears. I couldn't do anything. At the mercy of caregivers, I tried to minimize requests and remember to be courteous for what they did for me. I didn't want to be a pest. But oh, how I suffered.

Time stretched like pulled taffy. With nothing else to do, I scrutinized the busy nurses and their whining and complaining patients. I didn't want to add to their burdens. They already had to do everything for me from putting me on and off a bedpan, propping a pillow under my head, cutting my food into small bites, covering me with a blanket, washing me, and supervising my medical condition. Enduring this for three months made me feel like a two-year-old. I even cried like one. It was tedious and frustrating. I tried to keep reminding myself that good would result. I would be able to walk so much better. But it's tough when you're only ten years old.

Since the body cast severely restricted my movements, I became intrigued at visiting times with watching my roommate Peggy. She had normal speech and hearing, but she communicated by sign language with her deaf parents. I was absorbed in their animated silent conversations.

During slack times, Peggy agreed to teach me to finger spell using the Manual Alphabet and a few signs for common phrases. As I learned this new way of communicating, we happily engaged in baffling anyone who passed by or came into our room.

At the end of November, I was sent home to convalesce. Uncle Jack, a tall and handsome Irishman, delivered me in his station wagon. When he arrived at the hospital with my Dad, he took one look at me in my blue cocoon and all he could say was, "Holy Mackerel!" I laughed at his jokes when he and Dad carried me into the house. He not only lifted my heavily plastered body, but he lifted my spirits with his jovial nature.

Life was turned topsy-turvy at home. A makeshift sleeping area was made for me in a corner of the main room. I was centrally parked in the hubbub of everything. I was close to the Kalamazoo stove, the kitchen, the main eating area and the TV. It was better than being sequestered anywhere else in the house. For privacy when I used a bedpan or bathed, Dad rigged a draw curtain. It all worked out. I was thankful to be home.

When it was time to have the cast removed, I returned to the hospital and remained there for a week, as I worked hard in physical therapy so I could be mobile once again. When the cast was removed, I was left with a wicked-looking six-inch scar on my left hip. Most people would never see this part of my anatomy and could care less, but I cared. Still, I felt blessedly light when I was freed from the weight of the cast. I fervently hoped I'd never become obese. I hated the feeling of being a whale.

It was during this hospital stay that I encountered a friend of the devil. In the shadows of a Friday night, an eerie feeling woke me from a sound sleep and I found a pair of beady eyes staring at me through the hallway window.

Who is that? How long has he been gawking at me? What is he doing here?

Leering when he realized I was awake, he turned his head to take a side look down the long vacant hall. Then he swaggered boldly through the doorway wearing a white medical coat. Matter-of-factly, he pulled the privacy curtain closed, set his chart on the bed, switched on the overhead light and proceeded to boldly draw the sheet down to my feet, saying, "I'm here to take a look at you."

With my heart thundering wildly in my chest, I stared into his menacing eyes. Reacting defensively, I slammed at his hand as he started to lift my hospital gown. In a brave, clear voice I exclaimed, "Take your hands off of me. Go away now or I'll hit the call button and scream for Nurse Mullins."

Those evil eyes glared as he sucked in a deep breath. He actually hissed at me as his lips curled into a contemptuous smile. He dropped his hand to my inner thigh, quickly slithered it down to my foot, picked up his chart, pulled open the curtain, and stopped momentarily in the doorway to check the hall before sliding away.

Whew! I was mad and terrified. Why was he looking at me? Why did he creep in here in the darkness?

Shivering and trembling with fright, I covered myself back up. Tears started to leak out, but I brushed them away. My vulnerability had never been more plain. I couldn't get out of bed. I couldn't run away. No one was around to help me. And those wicked hands were not the hands of a healer.

I wanted the comfort of my mother's arms around me, but if I told her, I'd bring her more grief. She had enough burdens. If I told Nurse Mullins, she'd be upset. I didn't want to cause trouble. But I decided if I ever saw him again, I would say something to someone in charge. Until then, I'd keep it to myself.

In this catastrophic moment, I found I had God-given resources and strength. I had a voice that could speak, a sound mind, hands that had offset a bodily insult, and a spirit that didn't cower. Blowing my nose and drying my eyes, I thanked my guardian angel for protecting me. Once again, I prayed to Michael the Archangel to continue to give me courage.

After that night, I wanted to find solace, receive the Eucharist, and thank God for being with me at all times. I could attend Holy Mass on Sunday in the hospital chapel by making a request in advance for transport. I am forever thankful that the seeds of faith were planted early in my upbringing by my parents, watered by my grandparents, sprouted and nourished by my aunts, and eventually bloomed during my Catholic school education. I knew Jesus would help me heal in mind and body.

8

OPEN-AIR MEMORIES OF FRESH
AIR CAMP

ON A TUESDAY in July of 1953 as Mike pushed open the kitchen screen door he called out, "Mail delivery!" He deposited a bundle of mail on the table, but held a business envelope to the light. After scrutinizing it, he smirked as he airmailed it to me down the counter and exclaimed, "Sister, I have a feeling you're going to Hell."

Setting her knife down and wiping her hands on her apron, Mom pointed a finger at Mike. "Watch your language young man. You know better than to talk like that in this house." She glared at him, then returned her attention to the carrots she was slicing.

I glanced at the return address on the letter and sucked in a whoosh of air. I tore it open and spread several sheets over the counter top. "Mom, he's right! I'm going to Hell, Michigan, for two whole weeks! The Welcome-to-Camp letter has come!"

I scurried to the downstairs closet, dug out the family's battered brown suitcase, and opened it to air. Next, I pulled out a box with mom's sewing supplies and sorted through the pile of clean flour sacks, choosing some with pretty floral prints. laying them out for mom to look at. I envisioned the half-dozen shorts and tops she'd sew for me.

Starting when I was seven, the times I felt the most physically and emotionally whole occurred two weeks every summer when I could attend the polio camp funded by the March of Dimes. It was located near the small hamlet of Hell, Michigan, about a half hour from home. I cannot express how deeply grateful I am to the people who made the Fresh Air Camp available to us. The camp experiences lessened the burdens of hundreds of polio children and enriched their lives immensely.

Memories of my camp experiences shine in my mind like treasured charms on a charm bracelet. Those were the glorious days of my childhood. This one time of year, I could play and learn with others whose bodies had been ravaged by polio, giving me so many new insights. I attended camp for seven summers.

The staff of senior and graduate students representing the fields of education, social work, physical education, nursing and medicine, inspired a can-do attitude. Serving as our counselors, instructors, and role models, they made the impossible seem possible.

I loved watching teen boys cruising in wheelchairs while playing a game of basketball. I was impressed with their shooting prowess and how they could spin wheelies and stop on a dime. Games were played at a fever pitch. Their counselor, a pre-med student named Jim, ran the nature center and coached them as well. He, too, had polio. He walked with a limp, thanks to a weaker right leg. His example of optimism and normalcy encouraged me to consider options which I otherwise would not have tried.

Kids wearing leg braces stood on the archery course, hitting the target over and over. Everywhere I looked, campers hobbled on crutches, wheeled themselves in chairs, or limped, as they coped with paralyzed extremities. They rambled over the grounds participating in activities from morning until night.

The first skills our counselors taught us were ways to get along with others and forge teamwork. Before breakfast, a contest determined which cabin earned the coveted pennant for the neatest and cleanest. My roommates and I tried hard to win. We meticulously made our bunk beds, dusted, gathered wildflowers and displayed them in Coca-Cola vases around the room. We not only swept the cabin, but also the dirt walkway that led to the cabin, lining it with small rocks and writing the word WELCOME with small sticks. During breakfast, judges inspected cabins and announced the winner of the day over the loudspeaker. We always won the pennant at least once during our stay.

One of those mornings when tidying the cabin, I discovered a large dead moth on the window ledge. It was a rare find, striking not only in size, but in its showy coloring. I mulled over the idea of taking it to the nature hut to show Jim, the naturalist, but the hut scared me. From one quick peek through the doorway, I knew it housed gross stuff. I saw two frightening stuffed owls, jars of pickled leopard frogs, skeletons of woodland animals, and—to my horror of horrors—jars of Michigan snakes preserved in formaldehyde. I wanted nothing to do with the nature hut until I found this moth.

Summoning all my courage, I reluctantly took my find to Jim, who was well aware of my aversion to his favorite place. When I showed him what was in the box, he told me it was a spectacular specimen called a Cecropia moth. Coaxing me inside, he pointed to a poster of the moth family and suggested I start an insect collection. I avoided the shelves with the snakes, but my curiosity about the world of insects was so strong it helped me grow in bravery.

Marveling at the habits, intricacies, and diversity of these tiny creatures, I spent countless happy hours reading and discovering the insects' role on this planet. During my last summer of camp, I filled two Riker frames, one with moths and butterflies, and the second with a variety of other insects. Back home, I displayed them on my bedroom wall. They reminded me of an important lesson. No matter how small, each of us serves a purpose.

Campers all discovered and developed special interests and skills during those summers. Every day my cabin mate, Regina, headed to the Arts and Crafts Center, walking with two full-length leg braces. She also had an arm crutch that stopped just past her elbow, to help support her weak right arm. She kept a small pack at her waist where she collected treasures from nature like interesting stones, a bird feather, or pinecones. At the center, she'd slip on a wrist support that helped her hold a pencil, and drew lovely pictures of her small finds. Regina was just one of many who astounded and inspired me.

The crafts center contributed to my personal growth as well. There I was encouraged to tap into my artistic nature. I learned wholesome life-long habits and hobbies that sprouted a garden of happiness in my heart. Favorite projects included watercolor pictures, clay pots, woven bracelets and a colorful mosaic plaque of a sunfish.

I loved watching campers weigh their challenges and figure out how to transfer safely in and out of a rowboat before manning oars to head for a secret fishing hole. The smiles on their faces when they returned with their catches spoke volumes. Despite limitations, campers pondered possibilities, made choices, and acted upon them. We were "can-do kids" at camp.

We fished, canoed, and motor-boated through the chain

of lakes to observe wildlife in their natural habitats. And we all spent hours swimming. The sturdy sixty-foot, extra-wide dock accommodated wheelchairs and offered secure footing to children walking with crutches or an uneven gait. For many campers, these two weeks were the only time all summer we felt unfettered. Swimming gave relief from braces, and the exercises helped us relax overworked and painful body parts. The floating raft by the drop-off was used for sun-bathing, diving, and cannon-balling into the deep water.

During the last three summers of camp, we were supervised by a blond, suntanned lifeguard named Biff who was a favorite of us all because of his playful attitude and dynamic personality. He gave equal time to everyone, coaxing timid swimmers into the water and giving lessons for advanced swimmers.

Biff became my hero one late afternoon when the wind stirred suddenly, churning the water and bringing in dark clouds which blotted out the sun. Thunder rumbled loudly in the distance. Biff blew his whistle and called loudly, "Everybody out of the water now." He pointed a finger at me. "Ginger, get over here." Then he pointed to the ladder on the dock, reached out and gave me a swift pull to the dock. I turned my head to see a big black water snake glide inches from my shoulders as it disappeared under the dock and out of our swimming area.

I screamed and tears poured down my cheeks like twin waterfalls. Wrapping the beach towel around me, his big gentle hands hugged me and repeated, "Shush now, it's all right. That reptile just got lost in this rough water. He's back over in the rushes where he belongs."

I smelled his scent of Coppertone as my sobs turned into whimpers. I became embarrassed when I got hiccups and started to shiver. He toweled my hair dry while he said, "There, all the bad thoughts are gone. Now, get going." He pulled his blue sweatshirt over my head. It came down to my knees. He called my roommate, Linda. While rolling up the sleeves of the sweatshirt, he told us to high-tail it back to our cabin. And so, a traumatic incident ended happily.

On the last full day before returning home, we all posed on the raft in our bathing suits. Linda tried to hide her withered arm under the beach towel. I covered my bad left leg. Photographs were often distressing to polio victims.

Earlier, I was not happy when my brother Dick took a home movie of my other brothers and me playing ball in our backyard. I was so taken up with the game, I'd never spotted him on the sidelines filming us. I cringed when I saw myself making my way around the bases. I even hated looking at an x-ray of my spinal curve displayed on a lighted panel. I usually dealt with the problem of photos by using scissors to crop myself out of the setting. The camp picture was no different. "Ha!" Linda said. "You try to cover up your polio parts just like me, Ginger."

I nodded, admitting I felt betrayed by my body. "I think polio defines how others see me, especially if they don't know me." Linda said she admired me for not allowing the polio to depress or limit me.

"It's all in attitude," I told her. "My role model is the Black Angus."

"Wait a minute. What are you talking about? You've got to be kidding!"

I told her about my visit to our butcher shop, which has a poster of the Black Angus steer with the slogan: "Parts of me are excellent."

"Any time I feel bummed out about my self-image, I just say this like a mantra, over and over, and it makes me feel better. Parts of me are excellent."

On the final Saturday at camp, everyone participated in the farewell night big show. My cabin did a hammed-up rendition of the song "Side By Side." No matter their disability, everyone had a part to play in skits, songs, jokes, and comedy acts that poked fun at the counselors. We laughed so hard that our sides ached. Heading back to our cabins by moonlight and flashlights, we talked quietly, in groups of two-and-three. Others were silent, filled with their own private thoughts or just too tuckered out, but still glad to be in good company.

Suntanned, tired, and with my head full of treasured memories, I flopped into my bottom bunk and mentally rolled through the host of pictures in my mind. The next morning when I packed my bags, I knew I was taking home invaluable skills, talents, and ideas from this learning lab that I would use for a lifetime.

Later on, I learned about some of the history of the March of Dimes and the Fresh Air Camp. The National Foundation for Infantile Paralysis, which in time became known as the March of Dimes, was founded under the leadership of President Franklin D. Roosevelt and implemented by his law partner, Basil O'Connor in 1938. A polio victim himself, President Roosevelt was concerned with finding a cure for polio. Birthday Balls to celebrate Roosevelt during his birthday month of January were promoted by Hollywood to raise money for the March of Dimes. They became a huge success.

In 1946, as a tribute to Roosevelt on his birthday, his image was coined on the dime. Leeland Howard, the director of the US Mint, announced, "It is desired that the new dimes be produced at the beginning of the calendar year in sufficient quantity to use them in the infantile paralysis drive." Vaudeville star Eddie Cantor suggested the winning slogan for the campaign, "The March of Dimes." Basil O'Connor then formed a grassroots volunteer network that could raise money for polio education, patient care, and virus research that in time funded the promising Salk vaccine.

The best campaign was The Mothers March of Dimes in local neighborhoods, whose theme "Turn on Your Porch Light. Help Fight Polio Tonight" was particularly a winner. Between the years 1951 and 1955, $250 million was raised and the March of Dimes became a model for well-run private charities.

PHOTOGRAPHS

The Visel Children. Top Row: (l) Richard John, (r) Mary Francis. Middle Row: (l) Donna Jean, (r) Robert William. Bottom Row: (l) Michael James, (r) Virginia Marie.

The Visel Children. Top Row: (l) Charles Thomas, (r) Dominic Allen.
Middle Row: (l) Jerome Arthur, (r) Ann Theresa. Bottom Row: Paul
Thaddeus.

At the end of April 1951, I was released from the hospital on crutches with two full-length leg braces attached to orthopedic shoes. I refused the wheelchair, stood my ground, and walked to the car.

Frequent water therapy played an important part of my continued rehabilitation. Donna once challenged me to lead our younger brothers and little sister to the top of the water slide at the lake. I used my hand to raise my weaker left leg one step at a time. After that first attempt, it didn't take me long to reach the top.

Our children, David and Marietta, are best buddies. When they're together, the never lack for things to do.

Younger sister, Ann, was afraid to take the reins an
around the back field in the neighbors' pony car
confidently raised my chin and said, "Don't worry
go nice and easy."

My husband Eri

9

PUBERTY STINKS

IN APRIL OF 1958, when I was in sixth grade, Donna took charge of my twelfth birthday party. She invited not just girls, but boys too. She wanted to see how everyone had grown since the time she was our kindergarten teacher's helper. She planned the decorations, food, and games. Spin the Bottle caused quite a stir!

After the candles were blown out, the ice-cream and cake consumed, and the last guest gone, I fingered three strands of plastic Pop Beads—a pearly white, a light blue and a pale pink one. Each strand contained thirty beads. They were my favorite gift. I looked forward to putting them together and taking them apart in different sequences to fashion bracelets and necklaces. Like these beads, my classmates and I would be linked together and separated at different times in the future. We shared all our grade school years together at St. Joseph Elementary. But change was inevitable.

A week later, the nuns scheduled an afternoon session for the girls in my class, along with our mothers, to meet with the county nurse to discuss puberty. We were presented with a booklet called *You're A Young Lady Now*, saw a movie, drank punch, ate cookies, and were allowed to leave early with our mothers. On the way out, we picked up our complimentary Be Prepared Kit with a box of Kotex, a tube of Clearasil, deodorant, soap, and shampoo.

My girlfriends and I had shared whispers and giggles about the awkward subject. Several of us had older sisters and a thimbleful of knowledge. We had sprouted hair down there and under our armpits. Some had experienced itchy blooming buds and surprise growth spurts, much like asparagus that shoots up overnight.

A year and a half later, my "friend" made its initial debut at school one early afternoon, hitting me hard with flu-like symptoms. I was sent to the convent to have Mother Marie Dolores take care of me. Directing me to the bathroom, she said, "You'll find what you need in the second drawer. I'll call your mother to come." A short time later, while I was finishing a cup of tea in the convent kitchen, I heard the nun laugh her big Irish laugh when she answered the door and greeted my Mom. I later learned from Mom that she had never experienced this kind of a situation with any of her other pupils. She got a little nervous about it and Mom told her she handled it well.

Leave it to me not to have the ordinary, run-of-the-mill kind of periods. Dr. Burns, our hometown doctor, diagnosed me with dysmenorrhea. The symptoms were as dismal as the name. I had moody blues, sharp stomach cramps, fatigue, diarrhea, occasional dizziness, and vomiting. I learned to eat small healthy meals, relax, and get plenty of sleep. I made friends with an over-the-counter medication called Midol and a heating pad. To further counteract the physical problems, I stretched and swam at that time of the month.

Dad surprised me with his concern and compassion. He said, "Get outside and walk in the fresh air and sunshine. I bet it'll help. Your walking has improved so much since your last surgeries."

"Why do I have these oddball troubles, things that don't bother most other girls? Why does God have to pile it on me? It's not fair."

Mom hugged me. "Honey, change is a condition of life. Some changes are hard. You'll have to accept it and learn to live with it."

During the week following the onset of my first menses, Dad selected a sturdy maple branch from the woodpile. Lovingly, he whittled it, cut it to size, peeled off the bark, rounded off the bottom, and polished it smooth, revealing a grain that over time aged beautifully. Dad's affirmation and gift of a walking stick gave me the power to take charge of my situation. The stick spoke to me with the strength of its maker, saying, "Get going, girl!"

This walking stick, along with my full-length left leg brace, which was attached to a custom shoe, allowed me to cover a surprising distance all around the farm property on well-trodden paths. They improved my physical and mental disposition. Now I could walk almost a mile on the back road to a friend's house.

But overall, I thought this growing-up business was yucky.

AT TIMES POLIO made me feel alone, despite being surrounded by a big loving family, school, and church community. I seldom saw anyone with physical problems like mine outside the hospital. In my everyday life, polio was a solo journey that often caused me to feel like the Lone Ranger. However, the mask I wore was invisible. I was careful to keep all hurts to myself. I didn't have a Tonto in my life to share problems, predicaments and strategies. The

common physical problems facing other kids my age—
acne, wearing glasses or a broken bone from a sports injury
—were addressed in pre-teen and teen magazines. My
problems were never mentioned on those pages.

I had to strategize all my moves, from going out the
door to climbing into a car safely without slipping or
tripping, wondering if I'd arrive close to an entrance, and
figuring out if my destination was even accessible. I had to
determine if furniture was safe and sturdy, not too low to
the ground, and if it had arms to help me get up. I needed
bare tile floors that weren't slippery, throw rugs that were
skid-proof and free of clutter, dogs that wouldn't jump on
me, cats that wouldn't get underfoot. Minor challenges for
others seemed insurmountable obstacles to a disabled
person. I needed to be on guard constantly to prevent
unsafe or embarrassing situations.

Since I had no role models in my life, I thought I might
find answers to some of the more difficult challenges and
inspiration by looking to books. Middle school teachers
required many book reports, I searched for stories about
people who were physically challenged.

Our school library had books on lives of the saints and
other holy people, many of them plagued with a severe
disability. Blessed Kateri Tekakwitha, Lily of the Mohawks,
was for a time estranged from her tribe because her body
was heavily pock-marked and her eyesight ruined by
smallpox. Saint Therese of Lisieux, the Little Flower, died in
her twenties of tuberculosis after years of struggling with
exhaustion from coughing and breathing difficulties. Both
of these women learned that their sickness had potential for
divine grace. They became spiritually strong and were able
to remain joyful in difficult, even extreme, circumstances.
These women accomplished amazing things, not only for
themselves, but for others as well. Saint Therese was
proclaimed as a doctor in the church. Blessed Kateri became

beloved by her people because of her kind words and deeds. She lived an exemplary life.

In the book about her life as a blind and deaf person, Helen Keller once said, "Although the world is full of suffering, it is also full of the overcoming of it." She dedicated her adult life to starting schools for the blind, promoting Braille, helping blind children in desolate countries, and writing inspirational books.

On other hunts through the shelves of the library, I found fictional stories of people with physical disabilities. *Heidi* is a story of a young girl who lived in the Swiss Alps with her grandfather. She befriends Klara, a wealthy girl confined to a wheelchair by polio. Klara visited Heidi in the mountains and was encouraged to exercise and play in the fresh mountain air and sunshine. There, she ate healthy foods and was treated normally, rather than like a fragile, porcelain doll. I loved that tale.

Some fictional stories told of extremely deformed characters. *The Hunchback of Notre Dame, The Phantom of the Opera, Beauty and the Beast,* and *Snow White and the Seven Dwarfs* featured characters who were ostracized from society because of their disfigurements. Although disturbing, these books taught me that no matter what our circumstances, we have a choice about how we respond. We can become bitter or better.

I inherited a box of Nancy Drew mystery stories from a friend. What a fantastic surprise! Hard cover and in mint condition, this collection became my prized possession. The heroine of this series taught me about strength of character, the importance of asking questions, being determined, using your head and your God-given talent, and following an adventurous nature. I was hooked on books. As the educator Charles Eliot said, "Books are the quietest and most constant of friends; they are the most accessible and wisest of counselors and the most patient of teachers."

Throughout the elementary grades, I was an "A" and "B" student with usually a "C" in mathematics. It was easy to keep up with reading, writing, geography, religion, and spelling when I missed school, but math was more difficult. I received no tutoring when it came to this subject. At least, that's my excuse.

During lilac season, the last ceremony before grade school graduation was the May Procession to pay tribute to the Mother of Jesus. This celebration began in the grotto and processed into church. The first communicants led the entire school, with the girls dressed in their white dresses and veils and the boys in dress slacks, white shirts and ties. The eighth grade class processed last, leading the rosary and the singing. I followed my class, carrying the crown on a satin pillow. My cousin Kathy crowned Our Lady.

Before this special ceremony, I had to face the ever-growing dilemma of what to wear. Buying clothes had become a challenge. A soft yellow chiffon dress, purchased off the sales rack at Goodyear's Department Store in Ann Arbor solved part of the problem. When we left the store, Mom suggested we look next door in Muehlig's Dry Goods Store.

My eyes gleamed in appreciation as they roamed over the prints, colors and textures of the bolts of fabric lining the shelves. I could have stayed there all day imagining the possibilities, but Mom was on a mission. She headed straight down a side aisle, opened her shopping bag, and pulled out the dress. She found matching material. "Please cut off a half yard," she said to the sales girl. To me, she quietly said, "I'll drape this loosely over the back of your dress, sewing it in a soft Grecian style to camouflage the curve of your spine." I was so grateful.

Like many polio victims, I hated clothes shopping then and I hate it today. It is a chore. And no matter how well I take care of my clothes, braces poke holes in slacks, dresses, and skirts.

Sewing is actually much easier than shopping. For years, my talented Mom made most of my garments. My older sisters were both competent pianists and seamstresses, but unfortunately, I did not follow in their shoes. My feet and legs did not have the muscles to use the foot pedal on the sewing machine or the piano.

I struggled to accept the fact that I didn't have strong sexy legs or feet. Mom and my sisters are attractive women blessed with great legs. As a girl, I wasted countless hours wishing I had glamorous legs like theirs, able to wear sheer nylons and strut in high heels. When it comes to footwear, standard Buster Brown orthopedic shoes with a steel shank are simply unfashionable. Whenever I had regrets, I reminded myself that I could have been an amputee. I've learned to be thankful for what I have.

But, there comes a time when a young lady needs a pair of dress shoes. Luckily, Mast's sold a T-strap flat with a steel shank that was made by the Naturalizer Shoe Company that could be adapted for a brace. These were kept only for special occasions and were perfect for the eighth grade May Procession and June graduation.

AT LAST, AFTER MY PARENTS' twenty-three years of childrearing, Paul was toilet trained and no Visel was in diapers. Ann had grown well past my kneecaps. When the first week of summer vacation arrived, after my eighth grade year, Mom and Dad began taking trips to the magnificent Great Lakes with the younger half of the family, all six of us. I was the big sister of this group.

After an attendant filled the tank of Dad's sedan with gasoline—which cost twenty cents a gallon—washed the front and back windows of the car, and checked the oil, we were on our way. Our first Great Lakes camping trip took us 180 miles to the west side of the Lower Peninsula, to the city of Saugatuck on Lake Michigan. Though it was a workout, I climbed the 287 steps of Mt. Baldy, one at a time using the railing. Yes, determined to reach the top, I counted each step. When we were drawn to the sandy, white Oval Beach, I swam in the tingling cold waters of Lake Michigan with my family.

Our dune buggy experience with a professional driver was the highlight for everyone. We thrilled when we zoomed up and down over the great mounds of sand with the wind off the lake cooling our faces and whipping our hair. This experience reminded me of how it felt to run in the days before polio. I loved anything that went fast and emulated the feeling of running.

Soon after, Mom and Dad decided on a more daring adventure, a camping trip to the Upper Peninsula with me and my five younger siblings—Charlie, Dominic, Jerry, Ann, and Paul. Driving through the northern wilderness of the Lower Peninsula, we all shared the fun of reading the names of residences posted at the driveways of private properties, like X-scape Acre, Sunset Shores, Sail-Inn, Days End, Fish and Wish, and Kenny's Camp.

After a wonderful day visiting Mackinac Island, Ann got seasick on the boat ride back to our campsite. Once again on solid ground, she plopped under a shady tree, covered herself with a beach towel and snuggled down for a nap. The rest of us gleefully swam along the rocky shore of Lake Huron wearing old tennis shoes to protect our tender feet while Dad fished until dinnertime. I felt so alive and confident of myself physically, happy to be able to keep up with my brothers.

Dad cleaned the perch he caught, wrapped them in aluminum foil, and placed them on a rack over an open-pit fire alongside corn roasting in the husk and baked beans. Cantaloupe was dessert. From our vantage point we had a spectacular view of the Mackinac Bridge. It felt like Christmas in July at nightfall when the lights on the gigantic bridge lit up.

Here, in a small pop-up tent with my younger siblings all nestled together, I nodded off to sleep with the sound of the waves lapping against the shore. I felt so vibrant and strong after swimming, glowing with the warmth from the sun, and eating healthy food. I marveled at this immense water wonderland as I connected with Mom and Dad and half the family on vacation.

BACK AT HOME THAT SUMMER, I rambled around the countryside more and more, always feeling safer with my walking stick, except for one worry. Snakes. The mere thought of a snake still frightens me to death. Picking strawberries, green beans, tomatoes, or other produce in the garden, walking by the marsh to my girlfriend's farmhouse, or being in the orchard could turn into a nightmare if I happened to see a blue racer, garter snake, milk snake, or an ugly black water snake. Most everyone with me would yelp and scatter away, leaving me frozen in place. I was scared of falling and finding myself on the ground with the snake. Screams tore out of my mouth and I would sob until someone came to my rescue.

During one walk, Charlie and I were taking a shortcut through a field to our aunt's house when we met a big garter snake. Charlie swiftly chased it away and laughed at me when I started hollering. "Knock it off! Stop being a sissy!" he commanded. I wiped my tears away. Not twenty-five feet later we walked into a *nest* of garter snakes—a mother with several babies entwined around her.

"Oh, gross!" I yelped. Charlie had never seen anything like this before. His face went as pasty white as mine must have been. He hoisted me up piggy-back style and scrambled home.

Dad tried several times to reassure me about this fear. "Ginger girl, listen to me, those snakes won't harm you. They're afraid of you." Well, they sure fooled me. They made my skin crawl and gave me nasty nightmares in which I was always helpless and unable to escape. I reminded myself to pray, and have faith that Jesus would protect me.

SIXTEEN-YEAR-OLD MIKE WORKED full-time during this same summer of 1960, delivering furniture for a local store in the village. At the end of July, on the last stop of the day, he drove down a gravel road by a canal at Portage Lake and noticed a neighbor hammering a *For Sale by Owner* sign on the front lawn of his cottage. Mike asked the price and thought it was reasonable, so he encouraged our parents to buzz over and see this cottage. Mike was convincing. Mom said to Dad, "The Lord works in strange and mysterious ways. It won't hurt to take a look."

"Can I go too, please?" I asked.

The cottage was named *Rest-a-While*, announced in bold red letters on a white-and-green background attached to the peak over the front porch. "That saying is from the Gospel of Mark," Mom said quietly, staring at the sign. "When the apostles returned to Jesus after completing a mission, He told them, *Come away by yourself to a deserted place and rest a while.* I have a good feeling about this."

Dad and Mom loved the idea that it had lake access on the side road. They studied the layout of the white cottage. The big front porch and all the windows had red trim. The front and side doors were dark green. It seemed sturdy and welcoming. Dad said, "Okay, let's ask if we can take a look."

The owner offered a tour. We all scrutinized the small cozy kitchen with a hand pump, the living room with a fieldstone fireplace, a tiny bathroom, and two small bedrooms before sitting on a glider on the expansive screened-in front porch. As the adults discussed the price, I looked across the road at the canal where cottages could dock boats and discovered the lake and sandy beach nearby.

We bought the cottage. It became a blessing, providing our family with a retreat from the everyday world. It had always been a family dream to live by a lake. Everybody was proud of Mike for helping us transform a dream into reality.

My challenge for the remaining summer mornings was to swim all the way across the lake and back. Mom rowed the boat out of the canal and onto the lake. I slid out and began swimming across while Mom rowed alongside me. On the other shore, I played and rested in the warm sand, looked for shells and minnows, ate a piece of fruit, then swam back to the other side. It was a great workout for both of us. I swam so much that summer I felt I had grown gills.

Summer meant swimming, sliding down the big water slide, and diving or jumping off the raft. Sometimes on a weekend evening we built a bonfire down on the beach, roasting hot dogs, making s'mores, and just hanging out.

My disability didn't deter neighborhood kids from playing with Charlie and me. They were known as the Fox Point Kids. Monica, Cheryl, Tommy, and Ron were all city kids who came to the lake for the summer. Tommy, who lived the closest and attended our church, became our companion from late morning until early evening.

This particular summer, a lot of natural awakenings and

adrenaline were pumping through my age group. Tommy and Ron were showing a strong interest in me, much to Charlie's disdain. I liked Tommy.

One evening on Labor Day weekend, Charlie, Tommy, and I went fishing in Dad's rowboat. School would soon start and we wouldn't see Tommy until next summer. Charlie did most of the fishing. Tommy and I were fishing for something else.

Then Tommy stole a kiss! I assume he wanted to leave me with something to remember him by. Even though it was quick, Charlie still saw it. He took hold of the oar and splashed us both. That was my first kiss, and a big wet one at that. It was wonderful to feel young and alive, with a future full of promise. I had enjoyed two rare family camping trips, the adventures of acquiring a lake cottage, and a first boyfriend who promised to write. I felt bursting with happiness, a grand opening to my teenage years. I entered high school feeling hopeful and excited about turning the next corner.

THE CLASS OF 1964

Bravo! Father Sylvester Van Tiem carried the torch for parochial education and backed his words with actions. He offered transportation and tuition assistance to anyone from the graduating class of St. Joseph Grade School interested in attending St. Thomas High in Ann Arbor, a half-hour drive away. Mom and Dad took him up on his offer.

Dad worked the early shift at Hoover Ball and Bearing Company and left the house at 6:00 a.m. He was my alarm clock. He'd call softly, "Ginger Girl, wake up" from the bottom of the stairs. By the time he reached the top step, I was in a sitting position with the bedside lamp switched on low. He would deliver a steaming cup of hot coffee, kiss me, and whisper, "Have a good day." Since our upstairs was unheated, this warmed my heart and launched my day happily.

Dependable Uncle Mike, an electrician who lived on the back road behind our house, picked me up at seven o'clock on his way to work. He turned on the porch light when he went out his door, my signal to walk to the end of our driveway. He drove the 2.5 miles through Dexter, delivering me to our parish church twenty minutes ahead of the bus. I slipped inside the unlocked building, a haven from the cold, and had a precious pocket of time to pray before morning Mass.

In the darkened interior, the stillness filled me with peace, and the steady flame from the sanctuary light beckoned me forward. Sitting in a pew, I'd thank the Lord for the new day and ask to be open to any lessons He had for me and the grace to meet any challenges. Resting in His presence, before the day became filled with non-stop activity, was a special time.

Mr. Bell, a portly man with a good sense of humor, appeared at 7:30 a.m. in our yellow mini-bus. During the nine-mile trip, we all knew he cared about his cargo. He made everyone feel important. He showed an interest in our studies and cheerfully sent us off for our "book-learning time."

It was a gigantic step to leave our village and go to the big town of Ann Arbor. St. Thomas Catholic Church, not far from the University of Michigan's central campus, looked like a cathedral to me. Though feeling like a country bumpkin, I was pleased to follow in the tradition of my older brothers and sisters. "If they could do it, I can, too," I repeated to myself.

Going from a class of nineteen students to almost eighty was daunting. Freshmen girls reported to Homeroom 104, the boys to 106. After prayers, attendance, and announcements, classes began. My science class was on the main floor. All other classes were on the second floor. At the end of each class, I was allowed to leave five minutes early, before the bell rang and everyone spilled out into the hustle and bustle of the hallways. This gave me a head start and safe passage.

Getting to the cafeteria for lunch meant I had to negotiate two additional stairways through the elementary section of the complex, while the other high school students had to go outside regardless of the weather and walk down a steep hill, something I couldn't safely negotiate. By the time I entered the cafeteria, there was hardly a line. I filled my tray, ate, and then backtracked to the high school with enough time for a bathroom break.

Most St. Thomas students had been together since kindergarten. They were amiable and pleasant, but reserved. Because of the distance to Dexter, it was hard to include newcomers in many events, especially since we had to leave as soon as school adjourned since our bus was waiting. It took time to find our comfort zone and see ourselves as a unit.

Thanks to my older brothers and sisters who had graduated from St. Thomas, I knew some of the older students. I looked forward to study hall after a friendly senior, a commuter from Pinckney (twenty-nine miles away), chose a seat at my study table. He had visited our house a couple of times with my brother Mike. I was flattered that he acknowledged me. He was intelligent, a star athlete, and personable. He made me laugh and helped dismiss many of my fears. When he saw me in the hall, he smiled and said hello.

Later, he wrote in my yearbook words I never forgot. "Ginger, going over my days early in the fall brings me back to the time when we both were in the same study hall in the library. It sure was fun gossiping like old women. You have a bright future ahead, so keep it up. Best wishes, Jim."

Most instructors at St. Thomas were Sisters of the Immaculate Heart of Mary, the same order that taught me in grade school. A lay instructor, Mr. Thompson, taught science and biology. He was good friends with our next-door neighbor at the cottage, so we had something in common.

We also shared an interest in art. When he lectured, he'd

"chalk talk" with colored chalk, drawing animals, reptiles, and other creatures. He encouraged us to express ourselves artistically in our assignments. One memorable project was to choose an animal, write a report about it and use crayons to illustrate its life cycle on a 20x24-inch piece of muslin. We covered it with another cloth and ironed the area to make it more permanent. I chose the life cycle of the leopard frog. These amphibians fascinated me with their croaking and their big eyes bulging amongst the lily pads.

My two hardest classes were algebra, which I managed to plow through, and Latin, taught by Mr. Heilfrich. I knew the Latin prayers of the Mass, because this was before the Vatican II Council changed everything into English. But the only way I managed to make sense of the Latin assignments was to go next door to Grandpa's kitchen table. I did my homework under his tutelage. Grandpa had gone to St. Ignatius Loyola University and seminary for four years before deciding that the priesthood was not his true vocation. However, he knew his Latin. Suffering through his haze of cigarette smoke, I'm glad to report, I made the grade.

Monsignor Peek, a tall and large-boned man, looked regal in his clerical garb with his black cape lined with red satin. He walked on the sidewalks around the school, praying from his breviary, mingling with the students, sharing a laugh, talking sports, offering prayers, and listening.

The 1960s was the era of Rock and Roll music. To my delight, I was asked to the Homecoming dance my freshman year and the prom my senior year. Both of the boys were in my class. They had a good sense of humor and were genuinely kind people. I thought that if they had enough nerve to ask me out, then I should accept. Besides, I really wanted to go to these important dances.

Freshman year, Mom found royal blue satin material

enhanced with silver thread and fashioned a lovely knee-length dress, which complimented my corsage of pink sweetheart roses. At the senior dance, I wore a floor-length, pastel-blue formal with a tiara in my long blonde hair, and my date gave me a fragrant wrist corsage.

The slow dances were easy. Fortunately for me, rock 'n' roll allowed everyone to use their imagination while dancing. Chubby Checker said it best in his song "The Twist." "Round and round and up and down you go again..."

Other than those two highlights, most of my time was spent with four special girlfriends. I loved invitations for overnights for the independence from home. Sometimes we went for pizza after a movie or other events. When the weather was fair, I'd invite them out to the lake. But, in retrospect, despite these pleasant memories, my high school years felt like one hurdle after another. Rarely was there time for socializing between the long commute, homework, and my part-time jobs. The summer months opened up chances to relax with friends from the lake.

Sophomore year I was given a choice about further surgery on my left knee in an attempt to stabilize it so I could walk without a full-length leg brace. I desperately wanted to be free from all appliances. This decision meant that St. Thomas would be impossible for me to attend because of its barriers. I wouldn't be able to maneuver them while I was in a cast. The trip and the many flights of stairs would be too much. My plan was to return for junior and senior years.

For the first time ever, I attended a public school. Going from a strict parochial background to public school was an eye-opener. The biggest shock was life in the hallways. Students wove in and out any which way, sometimes running, dodging, and bumping into each other. Some hovered around lockers kissing, walking hand-in-hand, or entwining their arms around each other.

My biggest defense was the sight of me laboring with crutches and a cast, but I really did not feel safe in the hallways. I couldn't count on students to pay attention. I'd wait as long as possible after the bell rang so the students in my class could exit first. Then I made my way as close to the wall as I could to get to my next class. It was terrifying.

I was friends with a giggly group of kids from the lake. One day the teacher sent me—no one else—to the office for laughing loudly at a joke. I felt humiliated as I hobbled down to the office in tears. Our principal, nicknamed Mr. Mac, tried hard not to smirk when he heard my infraction. After his obligatory talk, I apologized, and then he asked me to wait outside his office for the rest of the period. I was the least of his problems, and I was probably the only student ever sent down for laughing.

Although the work load was easy and I did not have to endure grueling study times, I didn't participate in after-school activities. That aspect of teen life was shelved because I was not physically capable. When the school day was over, all I wanted to do was rest.

The end of the school year came and went and so did the leg cast. To my bitter disappointment, I learned that the surgery and sacrifices had been futile. The leg brace had to stay on. Even with the surgery, my knee muscles were not strong enough, so my knee continued to buckle. I knew there had been no guarantee of complete success, but I'd decided to try anything for even the slim possibility of throwing away my ugly brace, which dragged me down as effectively as a ball and chain. The medical community had tried its best to fix me.

Now there were no more options, no more hope of normality for this leg. Why couldn't I be like everybody else? I was devastated.

Granted, for the past few years, with the help of therapy, surgeries and many prayers, my right leg regained enough strength to be free of needing a full-length leg brace. On my left leg, I wore a brace with a lock on either side of my knee that ran all the way up to my hip with steel bars and leather bands around my thigh and calf. It would be a necessity for life. The full leather cap supporting my knee would be replaced with lighter straps, but that was the only concession.

Many students never knew about my polio. They assumed I had broken a bone and I'd be good as new once the cast came off. It wasn't unusual to see an athlete in a cast and on crutches. But I was stuck with the brace and a limp for life.

It was so hard for me to learn to accept that everything doesn't always work out the way we hope or expect. I cried a ton of tears. I pulled into my shell and sank into self-pity, distancing myself and ranting at God for about a week or two. I got all my anger and frustration out, and then decided to get over it and face my options. Things could be worse, I knew. I focused on all the things I was able to do and became determined to do the best I could with God's help and with the challenges I had been given.

That summer, I took driver's education. Every other sixteen-year-old I knew was going for their driver's license, too. The rite of passage implied more independence. I passed the course and finished the driving tests with flying colors after a drive around our village, which had no stop lights, and a drive on the country roads. However, in my heart of hearts, I knew that my leg reflexes were not quick enough to hit the brake fast in a real emergency.

In good conscience, I knew I had to forego applying for my license. Here was another roadblock staring me in the face. Had my chance of ever attaining a license been hijacked? I felt like a flat tire. This was even more difficult to accept than my failed surgery. I was frightened when I thought I'd have to rely on alternate means of transportation for the rest of my life. That decision gnawed away at my sense of ever being fully independent. Over and over again I asked the Lord, "Whatever is to become of me?"

Deciding to return to St. Thomas for my junior year, I took a summer babysitting job with neighbors at the lake in order to pay for tuition and books. The position was ideal. I was a mother's helper for three children, ages seven, five, and two. In the mornings, I was responsible for the seven-year-old boy and the five-year-old girl on the beach. I enjoyed teaching them to swim. In the afternoons, we would have a quiet time reading books or playing card games while the baby girl took a nap. Also, the parents were members of the yacht club and raced their Rebel sailboat, attended various club meetings, and partied afterward. I babysat a lot.

As the school year began, I learned that our new pastor had eliminated the bus service and tuition support. It took some juggling to work out rides to school. Luckily, I became friends with a dark-haired, brown-eyed girl named Terry, whom I met in French class. Not only was she a straight "A" student who spoke beautiful French, she also lived just a few blocks from the school. Her mother, a single parent, worked full time as a legal secretary, arriving home about 5:30 or 6:00 p.m.

I got to know her mom and her three rambunctious younger brothers early in the school year. Her mom noticed how I interacted with the younger boys, acting as a buffer between her daughter and her sons. She asked if I would be interested in a job as a helper to her daughter after school. Since I had to wait for my ride home, I was glad for this offer. Pitching in to help with the boys was no trouble. Together, Terry and I supervised their activities, practiced our French, and kept things in good order.

Terry impressed me with her ability to get dinner in the oven before her mother came in the door. Watching her in the kitchen gave me confidence about cooking. Meanwhile, she was impressed with my ways with her brothers. Growing up with seven brothers and their friends gave me a lot of practice. Being raised in a male-dominated environment, I wasn't fazed by boys. Her brothers obeyed me without any objections.

Like me, Terry had challenges—just different ones. Terry was a problem-solver who had to deal with real life issues at an early age. Despite the huge responsibility put on her shoulders, she was cheerful, fun to be with, and mature beyond her years. I vowed to be the same.

During my senior year, I learned that God answers many kinds of needs. The typing teacher, Sister Marie Celine, asked if anyone was interested in a job working in the business office at St. Joseph Mercy Hospital from 2:30 until 5:00, and Saturdays at the reception desk. I raised my hand, filled out the form, went for an interview, and was hired. I was elated! In good weather, walking the few blocks from school up to the hospital was doable. The few times it was too snowy or icy, I called for a cab. I contributed $2.00 a week in gas money to catch a ride to St. Thomas with a young woman who passed right by my driveway on her way to work in Ann Arbor. A neighbor lady who worked in the business office drove me home. I was getting a real paycheck. This job paid for tuition, clothes, and lunch money. What was left went into a small savings account.

Work and education were preparing me for more responsibility. I began to seriously consider going to college, perhaps even becoming a teacher. I had interacted and enjoyed being with my younger brothers and sister and their friends all my life, and I'd done enough babysitting to know I was patient with children. I thought God was steering me in this direction. I prayed for His guidance.

Graduation day pumped me full of triumph for what I had already achieved. Looking at my fellow graduates, I could feel their sense of pride too, and recalled the quote by Kahlil Gibran, posted above the chalkboard in our senior homeroom. "Work is love made visible … And all work is empty save when there is love." We had all completed difficult work that had helped form and shape us.

At the entrance to the church, the graduating seniors lined up by height, gowned in our class colors, girls in white and guys in royal blue. When the organ pumped the strains of "Pomp and Circumstance," I whispered a prayer of thanks. We were on the threshold of a new chapter in our lives. This would be our last hour together before we took the plunge individually into the adult world. My classmates and I filed down the aisle behind the class officers to claim diplomas for the Class of 1964. I had no idea what the future would bring me, but I was anxious to find out.

PRAY, PLUCK AND A LITTLE BIT OF LUCK

THE SEARCH for an accessible college seemed to take forever. During the summer of 1964, I continued working at St. Joseph Mercy Hospital and visited colleges and universities in Michigan. I found acceptance academically, but not physically. There were too many physical barriers on campuses everywhere.

Parking was a nightmare no matter where I went, and besides, I couldn't drive. Some college students took a bus from their residence and were dropped off in a central spot. From there they did a lot of walking with a step at every curve and in all kinds of weather. Classes were in a variety of buildings with time constraints in between. I knew I couldn't do that. Entrances with steep steps and without railings were impossible for me to negotiate. A lack of elevator access added to the frustration. This was twenty years before the adoption of the Americans with Disabilities Act.

All my friends talked endlessly and excitedly about their college plans. But my dream of college looked bleak. I remained silent and heartbroken. I felt so lost, so discouraged by the unfairness. Dad told me to be content with the job I had in the business office at the hospital, but that didn't help.

Dad had always run hot and cold about the advantages of higher education. I tried to understand why he thought this way. His father had died when he was four years old. By the time Dad completed grade school, his formal education ended. He needed to go to work on the eighty-acre Visel family farm to help provide for his younger brother and sister. He had opted for the job in hand rather than the far-off degree. Considering my circumstances, he probably thought he was protecting me from further disappointment. He must have thought it was a delusion for me to think I'd find a college that would work. Anyway, there was no money for tuition. His advice remained, "Keep your job. It's a respectable place to work and has good benefits."

I stubbornly refused. I did not want to settle for a secretarial job. Thank goodness Mom agreed with me. Again and again, she reminded me, "If it's the Lord's will, He'll help you find a way." Then she reminded me to pray. *"Trust in the Lord with all thine heart, and lean not unto thine own understanding. In all ways acknowledge Him, and He shall direct thy paths."* (Proverbs 3:5-6.)

After yet another disappointing visit, this time to Siena Heights in Adrian, Michigan, the sister in charge encouraged us to visit Madonna College in Livonia. This college was building a residence hall with a short level walkway to the main academic building.

We made an appointment with the registrar, Sister Remigia. Yes, the campus would work for me once the residence hall was built, she said, but it wouldn't be ready until the next school year. She suggested that rather than delay going to college for a year, I should consider trying Marymount Junior College in Boca Raton, Florida. "It has an accessible campus with a central academic building and dormitory. And you wouldn't have to be concerned about walking in ice and snow," she told us. Until that moment, I had never considered looking outside Michigan because of the extra expense in going to school out of state.

With a letter of recommendation from her, I applied, and was accepted for the fall term. Now I had to contend with the ways and means to finance my education. The Lord had gotten me this far, and I continued to place my trust in Him and ask for guidance. I felt encouraged about the fact that it was a Catholic college named in honor of Mary.

Once again, Divine Providence supplied what I needed. When my Great Aunt Kitty died we learned that she had bequeathed a small inheritance to each of her grand-nieces and grand-nephews, giving us a chance to jumpstart our own personal dreams. It was enough for me to cover the first year's tuition.

The day after Labor Day, I boarded a jet for my first flight from the peninsula of Michigan to the peninsula of Florida. I was leaving the known—which could be scary— and heading into the unknown—which might be terrifying. After buckling up in my seat by the window, I waved good-bye to Donna and Mom, who were crying because I was going so far away from home. But I was all smiles, brimming over with joy. By God's grace, with prayer, pluck and a little bit of luck, I was on my way.

I already had lots of practice being separated from my family during hospital stays. This was a happy occasion, for once, to justify the separation. As the plane surged down the runway, I watched the familiar landscape zoom by with my heart full of great expectations. At long last, I was following my dream. My sister, Frankie, a graduate of Eastern Michigan University and an elementary teacher, had fought her own battles to achieve her dream. If she wanted a higher education she had to pay her own way. In her junior and senior years in high school she had various jobs in Ann Arbor after school and weekends and worked summer vacations at Newport Beach Club to put money away for college. After graduation, she worked a whole year full-time at a secretarial job and bought a used car. For most of that time she lived at home and then commuted to EMU and put her money toward tuition. She accomplished her goals. I now believed I was beginning to realize mine.

The sun blazed and the palm trees waved hello as the plane landed at the Miami airport. Another student and I boarded the limousine that had been arranged by the school. The driver loaded our luggage for the forty-five minute trip to the college.

Sister Mary Joseph welcomed us and asked if we would like to be roommates. We agreed. We walked through a large outdoor sitting area fitted with benches and surrounded by splashy flowers and lush greenery. Overhead, blue skies peeked through the vine-covered slats as we walked down a pea-pebble walkway to the entrance of the dormitory.

Sister assigned us to the last room next to the exit. "It'll serve as a shortcut when going to the academic building, the chapel, and the administration building."

Rooming with Arlene was great except for one thing. I was jealous of all the long letters she received from her father, who wrote to her every other week. Her spirits soared when she received these letters. She read each one out loud to me. They made her so happy. I had to hide how sad they made me. My Dad never wrote me a letter or sent me a card in my life. That left me with an ache in my heart.

I befriended Martha, a young lady from Coral Gables, Florida. Her family was originally from Cuba. She was a short, dark-eyed beauty. She loved art, music, and dance, and became my favorite friend. Martha enjoyed the freedom of living on campus and escaping the tradition of being accompanied by her nanny or her parents whenever she went out. At home, that was the standard practice for a single girl in her culture. Her boyfriend drove up from Miami some weekends, and they would go out on a date without her parents' knowledge. They were crazily in love.

One boring Saturday at the end of September, Martha talked me into getting my ears pierced. She felt capable of performing this minor operation, assuring me, "It's a piece of cake. In my family, it's tradition to pierce the ears of an infant girl before her first birthday." Back in Michigan, I didn't know anyone with pierced ears. She sterilized a needle with a flame and rubbing alcohol, iced my earlobes, took a ball point pen and made dots where she would pierce with the needle. After I drank about half of a bottle of wine—I still don't know where she got it—Martha said, "It's time to operate." I sat on my hands and held my breath. The needle slipped right through with no pain and no problem.

"Are you all right?" she asked.

"Sure," I replied in a confident voice, "after so many surgeries, ear piercing is no big deal." I silently congratulated myself that I hadn't fainted yet.

Actually, Martha was a little shaky. She took a deep breath and said, "Hang on."

The other ear was a little trickier. Martha got the needle half-way through and stopped. In a panicky voice, she said, "This is a tough ear lobe."

Taking command, I replied, "Okay, just give it one hard push." She did.

Quickly fitting a pair of gold studs into my ear lobes, she stepped back and admired her handiwork. She picked up a mirror and suggested, "Take a peek." Wiping the perspiration from her forehead, she exclaimed, "Pretty cool, huh?"

I considered this an initiation into adulthood, establishing my independence. I was my own person.

Classes were both interesting and challenging. I especially liked the World Literature in Translation class, which introduced important readings from other cultures. The text weighed close to five pounds. It was too heavy for me to lug around to classes all morning, so I left it in my dorm room. When references were made to a specific piece of literature, a friendly classmate shared her copy with me.

The other class I favored was Philosophy in Education. Here I first learned about Maria Montessori and her hands-on approach to learning. She was a physician treating special-needs children. Later, she worked with children from impoverished backgrounds at her school Casa dei Bambini (House of Children) in Rome. She believed children benefited from early education when they worked in an enriched, mixed-age environment, and learned at their own pace and interests. Her methods and philosophy excited me and later greatly influenced my teaching.

Opportunities for extra-curricular activities filled my spare time with purpose. I was a reporter for the campus paper called *L'AZUR* and served as secretary for the Future Teachers Club. Off-campus, I gained field experience teaching catechism to migrant children on Sunday mornings.

The migrant camp was five miles from the college. The main crop harvested at this time was tomatoes. Off to one side of the fields was a metal Quonset hut reminiscent of an airplane hangar. Inside, a makeshift altar with a white linen cloth covered the table. Candles and a vase of flowers were set for Holy Mass. After Mass, students in grades one through four met in separate classrooms partitioned with shower curtains. Each class had a portable chalkboard and metal chairs.

The children had varying degrees of proficiency in

English. They wore hand-me-down clothes and had sweaty, earthy-smelling bodies. However, their eager, direct looks and bright smiles were captivating. Going to the camp was a highlight of each week. On my last visit, my students presented me with a box of beautiful red tomatoes.

During Christmas break, I traveled back to Michigan, not by jet, but by Greyhound bus. Bless my brother Bob for paying sixty dollars for a round-trip ticket so I could go home for the holiday. What an experience. Looking out the window in the rural, snow-covered landscape, I saw many dwellings lumped onto the mountainsides with columns of smoke curling from the chimneys into the cheerless gray sky. Scantily clad people split wood by meager woodpiles. A man slopped a few hogs. One woman took frozen laundry off the line. A teenage boy and his dog hunted for game. School children were dropped off on a lane from an old dilapidated school bus.

The Greyhound bus stopped at all the big cities on the slow crawl from Fort Lauderdale to Ann Arbor. An assortment of characters got on and off. One tired old granny, with a plaid wool scarf tied over her hair and several teeth missing, sat down next to me. She quietly opened a wicker lunch basket and gummed her lunch of fried chicken legs and biscuits, after which she went sound asleep, snoring softly. I wondered about her story and those of several others. This was a tough, tiring trip, but worth it because it provided opportunities to observe and study the human condition in ways new to me. I had many hours to think. I felt badly for the international students who had to stay on campus and couldn't go home for Christmas. It made me appreciate the sacrifices they made to get an education. I realized I would never have to look far to count my blessings.

Summer arrives early in Florida. With three friends pooling resources, we spent spring break in Fort

Lauderdale. We sunbathed and swam with Beatles music blasting on the transistor radio. It wasn't too long before we paired up for a time with four college guys from Connecticut. They were a healthy, wholesome group, and we enjoyed each other's company as we partied by sunlight and moonlight.

Here I found acceptance in spite of my disability. Evidence of my polio is not something I can really hide. I learned not to sit back feeling sorry for myself. If I couldn't play beach volleyball, I could cheer my friends on as loudly as anyone. Some friends didn't go in the water. I love the water. I may not be a great dancer, but I could swim, sing songs and play guitar. I learned that attitude is critically important.

All too soon, June arrived, and I was back on the plane to Michigan. College brought me tremendous growth in confidence, enriched by friends from different cultural backgrounds. I gained a stronger conviction that teaching was the right career choice for me.

In the fall, I transferred to the teacher preparation program at Madonna College in Michigan. The new residence building allowed easy access to classes. I was awarded a full scholarship for the next three years. Once again, I made new friends and settled into the life of a student.

Although it was daunting to find myself on another new campus with a heavy workload, I took inspiration from Peggy Wood, who played The Mother Superior, and sang the powerful song "Climb Every Mountain" in the Rodgers & Hammerstein production of *The Sound of Music*. She reminded me of the Mother Superior who taught choir in my grade school. Whenever I needed a boost to climb what seemed to be another mountain, I'd sing those lyrics in my mind. That would free my heart.

During the next three years, most days were spent

between the dormitory and the academic building. If I wanted good grades, I had to work hard. For supplemental income, I worked in the dormitory at the front desk, greeting guests, fielding calls through the switchboard, and managing other business. Once a week, I had a commitment at Our Lady of Providence working with a small group of mentally impaired children—socializing, doing art projects, playing board games, and reading stories. This experience encouraged me to learn more about special education.

On weekends, I dated a boyfriend from Livonia. His family had a cottage on our lake. At Madonna, we attended Sunday Mass together, went out for pizza, to the movies, and to parties with friends from his school. We had a lot of things in common, especially our background connection to the lake. Second semester of my senior year, we broke off our two-year relationship. He was looking for a more permanent relationship. I was not ready for such a commitment.

I knew that when women marry, we marry the family as well as the man, and I suspected that his family, especially his mom, could not get past my disability. She was the kind of person who made me feel limited, that a woman with polio should not aspire to certain things— marriage to her son and having children being some of them. But, in reality, I knew I was way too young for marriage and wanted to continue enjoying my freedom and independence and dating and going to parties and being free to fly.

My best friend from high school, Terry, had gotten married earlier in the semester. As her maid of honor, I seriously considered this big step. My friends were all engaged, but I knew I wanted to do many more things before I made that choice.

DURING THE SECOND semester of senior year, the last eight weeks were dedicated to student teaching. I faced a major dilemma. I did not have a car or a driver's license. Most student teacher candidates had their own vehicles and were placed in the local schools in Plymouth and Livonia. I was distressed. There was no way I was going to be placed in a classroom near the college. Father Minck, the American Director of PIME Missions in Memphis, Michigan, was a real prayer partner. He interceded for me and told me things would work out. "Just keep the faith".

When my great Aunt Pearl heard of my problem, she invited me to stay in her lovely brick home in St. Clair Shores, just east of Detroit. She believed I could serve as a student teacher in her parish school, St. Clare of Montefalco, just two blocks from her home, which would be an easy walk for me. After speaking with the Mother Superior and the student teaching advisor, arrangements were made.

My widowed great Aunt Pearl was a faith-filled, dear old soul, with expressive, twinkling blue eyes magnified by her corrective lenses and rosy red apple cheeks. At home, she dressed neatly in a housedress and bib apron and wore her curly white hair short. Her jolly laugh spread good will. All through my childhood, she had remembered my birthday and other occasions with a cheery card, personal note, and a crisp new dollar bill. Whenever I was hospitalized, a card would come from her, again with a dollar bill enclosed as a "cheer-up treat." Now, at the end of my college years, she played her most important role yet, by opening her home and a teaching opportunity to me.

While I lived with her, she took on a significant project. She taught me to cook. In her spanking clean and organized kitchen, she sat with me at the table while we planned weekly menus with foods that I liked, and then made a grocery list. Once she phoned her order to the corner grocery store, the foods were delivered to her door.

Before the actual cooking was underway, she reviewed the recipes and explained her cooking methods. Under her tutelage, I turned out tasty old-fashioned dishes, like corned beef and cabbage, meatloaf, and pepper steak. Cooking for two was fun. I grew in confidence when it came to cooking. Since this great aunt never had children, I think she enjoyed these lessons as much as I did. For the first time in my life, I was treated like an only child.

She made me chuckle when she tried to play matchmaker. Now that she knew I could cook a decent meal, she wanted me to invite her twenty-eight-year-old bachelor neighbor to dinner. He was a handsome Irishman with a charming personality and she had known him all through his growing-up years. He had been her paperboy and shoveled her drive and walkway in the wintertime. After attending seminary for a number of years, he had returned to teach at the parish school. My great aunt tried her best to set us up, explaining he was a great catch. Although he was a fine fellow, I told her that he was too old for me. In later years, he became a priest.

While staying with her I was able to care for her ulcerated leg. After all, I'd been on the receiving end of nursing attention to my own legs. The wound was the size of a quarter above the ankle. I washed the open sore with hot water and Boric Acid, applied an antibiotic ointment, and replaced the dressing every day. This allowed me the opportunity to serve as a caregiver for a change.

Although Aunt Pearl, my Grandma's sister, never was able to have children due to miscarriages, she played an important role in the life of another niece and godchild, Mary Leonard, who had died of polio at the age of sixteen, many years before I was born. She dearly loved this girl. It seems such a shame that this bright, blue-eyed girl with the short cropped curly hair and big smile had her life snuffed out so tragically. Aunt Pearl had also supported my mother in her early childhood after her father died. Now, in her eighties, my great aunt took me under her wing. We both felt blessed.

St. Clare of Montefalco Elementary School was a private school with children from privileged homes. The girls wore blue plaid jumpers with white blouses. The boys wore dark dress slacks, white shirts, and ties. They learned at an early age that school was a place of business. I was assigned to second grade with Sister John Chrysostom and her thirty-eight students. At first, it appeared to be a gargantuan challenge. Self-doubt whirled in me. Thankfully, discipline was not a problem. High expectations of good behavior were the norm. These children came from homes where education was valued. Many were eager and competitive learners. Right from the start, I needed to be on my toes.

During the month of May, I was teaching full-time and responsible for a major end-of-the year project. My master teacher had emphasized, "When you have a choice, teach about what you love." I built the project around one of my favorite themes, our home state of Michigan. Inch by inch, I grew in confidence, flourishing under the wise and inspiring tutelage of Sister John Chrysostom. I felt the sweet bliss of success envelop me whenever a student experienced a light-bulb moment, reinforcing the truism, "It is in giving that we receive." In this first classroom, I determined to become the best teacher I could possibly be.

Before my college graduation, I had learned to teach in a wide variety of situations. I'd offered religious education to impoverished children in the migrant camp in Florida, worked with the emotionally and mentally disturbed as a "Big Sister" in Plymouth, and then with privileged second graders in St. Clair Shores. I felt ready for a full-time teaching job.

Graduation day arrived in May of 1968. It was an emotionally charged time filled with happiness, sadness at leaving my friends, great expectations for new beginnings, and thanksgiving for attaining goals thus far. However, the best part of the day was the sight of Mom, Bob, and my best friend, Terry, at the commencement ceremonies, along with, incredibly, Dad! After four years, he stepped onto campus. I finally felt validated.

IN THE DRIVER'S SEAT

"LADIES AND GENTLEMEN, this is your captain speaking. We
will be landing soon." Craning our necks to look out the
Pan Am jet window, we witnessed the first rays of the sun
burst over our destination, rewarding us with its textured
beauty. The land mass was a quilt of multi-hued greens,
edged in white lace. The dull gray winter was behind us
and a welcoming bright spring lay before us. Mom turned
to me chirping, "Top O' the Mornin', Kiddo." All the while,
our seatmates snored contentedly, oblivious to the captain
speaking or the miracle going on thousands of feet below.
We continued to gawk as we drew closer and closer to the
runway, our spirits awakening to new beginnings and new
adventures.

The trip came together during the springtime of 1968,
when I was happily entering my early teaching career and
Mom was close to her AARP years. She had a strong
yearning to visit Ireland, the land of her ancestors. I shared
her enthusiasm. On the tail-end of a long winter, we were
feeling stifled, like plants in a too-small pot. We needed to
stretch ourselves and grabbed at this opportunity to grow.

We discovered the Washtenaw County Catholic Deanery, which sponsored pocketbook-pleasing travel packages for parish members. The trip promised metropolitan and rural exposure. A priest accompanied the group to offer daily Mass and serve as a spokesperson when visiting areas of religious significance. Thankfully, the trip fell during my Easter break. This allowed us to celebrate our birthdays, exactly one week apart, abroad. With our passports in one hand and airline tickets in the other, we were launched.

Mom and I have a history of good times together and were as close as two birds in a nest. Now, I saw Mom with my adult eyes and sometimes I took charge in these foreign lands, causing her to see me in a different light as well. Our mother/daughter relationship reached new heights and depths as we grew in these shared experiences.

Did I have qualms about traveling to unknown lands and worry about how I'd manage getting around? Sure, I did. I wondered if I might be stuck at the hotels. Maybe the day trips weren't designed for someone with mobility issues. Would I be able to keep up with the group or suffer from fatigue and exhaustion? How far is too far? How much is too much? Lots of the challenges and concerns involved *stairs*, from a single deep step to lots of stairs without a railing, or stairs that were steep. Distance walking also loomed huge, especially up and down hills, walking on old cobblestone walkways, brick streets, and paths with rough terrain or gravel. I hoped to cope.

I decided to take these concerns on one at a time, use good judgment and go from there with trust and a prayer. And I did.

After conquering the three steps into the bus outside the airport, my concerns about getting around started to fade. I was pumped and ready for the challenges. By holding firm to the railings on either side of the entranceway, I pulled myself up. Claiming the first seat behind the bus driver afforded me extra room to avoid leg cramps. Exiting, I held tight to the guardrails and hopped down the steps, letting my arms do most of the work. The five steps at the entrance of our hotel also had sturdy rails, making for a safe entrance. Mom and I settled into our room, ate lunch, and decided to take a walk during our free afternoon to orient ourselves and work out kinks from our long flight.

In the sophisticated heart of Dublin, the fine 18th-century architecture was impressive. Most streets were level, sometimes brick or cobblestone, and lined with quaint black lampposts. The people dressed in smartly tailored clothing made from wool and linen. Their shoes, brief-cases, and purses were leather. Some carried an umbrella tucked under their arm.

Finding ourselves at Trinity College, we took time to visit the famous Book of Kells, then collapsed on a bench under a large tree to rest and observe our new surroundings. Here, even the students were smartly dressed. It shocked me when Mom stated, "I feel like a dowdy American, dressed in tennis shoes and a polyester pantsuit."

Taking another route back to the hotel, we rounded a corner where Mom was approached by a little ragamuffin with tangled red hair, saying, "Begging your pardon, Mum, could you spare me some coins for food? And I'm making me First Communion this coming Sunday. I'm in need of some new shoes." The little missy just didn't button her lip. She continued to rattle off a litany of needs.

"Come on, Mom. Leave her be," I called, as I kept walking away. But Mom continued listening to the child's woeful tale. And then she did what I hoped she wouldn't do. She reached into her purse and handed the waif a couple of bills.

"Oh, no, big mistake," I murmured.

Grabbing the money, the girl cheerfully sang her praises, "O' thank you, Mum. God bless you, Mum. Thank you, thank you." And she ran lickety-split out of sight.

"What do you make of all that? How pitiful. How could you ignore her?"

"Mom, you know the guide book tells us not to give money to beggars. We've also been warned by our tour group leader to pay them no mind. She's just playing with you."

About two blocks from the hotel, I knew we had run into another hot spot when a pack of street urchins popped out of nowhere. They took one look at me walking with a limp, and wearing a brace, and immediately circled Mom instead. They began pleading like hungry baby birds with their mouths wide open chirping their sad plight. Suddenly, Mom looked across the street and caught sight of the little redhead laughing at her as she peeked out from behind a bush, watching her partners in crime. Knowing she'd been duped, Mom took hold of her purse strap and put it on her shoulder. Holding it tightly, she marched with determination through their ranks telling them, "Stop bothering me or I'll call the police."

I'm glad this incident happened in the early part of our travels, as begging is a common practice in many countries of the world. From that moment on, Mom vowed to make all her charitable donations through her home church and her favorite foreign mission.

During the formal dress evening in the Banquet Hall, Mom had a chance to show her glam side. She wore a turquoise silk dress she had painstakingly fashioned from material Charlie had sent her when he served in Vietnam. While harp music played in the background and a waiter dunked her tea bag, steeping it to her preference, she looked at me and sighed, "I feel like a celebrity with all this special treatment."

"Well, I should think so. You certainly don't look like a dowdy American tonight." I teased.

The next morning, the pampering continued with a rap on the door and a voice calling out, "Room Service." I had secretly arranged for this special wakeup call for every day of our vacation. As a child, I had never, ever served Mom a treat in bed on special days such as Mother's Day or her birthday like a lot of other kids. I couldn't carry a tray up the flight of stairs to her bedroom without spilling or dumping everything. Now, what a golden opportunity to witness her surprise and see her being catered to in high style as the waiter set the tray by her bedside, opened the drapes to welcome the sun, and poured her a steaming cup of coffee from a silver pot, served with warm pastries as if she were someone rich and famous. Oh, how she glowed.

We connected with our Irish roots in the sixteenth century Abbey Tavern as we sat by a low burning turf fire and ate a hearty meal served with Guinness. Soon we found ourselves singing along with the Abbey Tavern Singers and their traditional instruments.

The light dimmed and shivers from the past swept through me when a soloist with a low haunting voice that seeped into the marrow of my bones sang, *"Too Ra Loo Ra Loo Ral."*

That song has resonated in my soul since the earliest days of my childhood when I was in so much pain, quarantined in University of Michigan Contagious Hospital. When Mom came to visit me, she was disguised from head to toe in a white surgical gown, mask, hat, gloves and paper slippers over her shoes. The only way I recognized her was by her eyes and her voice. I will never forget the helplessness I saw in those eyes when I begged her to make me better and take me home. Although she wasn't allowed to touch me, she sang this same lullaby. Oh, yes, now my eyes puddled. Looking across the table at her, she too was teary-eyed. We both knew what brought the tears. Whispering, she said, "You've come a long way, Baby. Strong as you ever were, strong as I knew you would be."

"Thanks, Mom, for all your faith and fortitude in putting up with me."

Motoring through the countryside by the lakes in Killarney, with hilarious non-stop banter from our bus driver, we stopped to shop along the way. I was passionate in persuading Mom to take this opportunity. I promised her she wouldn't go home feeling like a dowdy American. Once again, I found myself preaching, telling her we should splurge on some things we love. Every time we wore them, it would bring back great memories. We each bought fisherman sweaters with knit hats and Connemara marble gold earrings. It wasn't often that I'd play this role reversal, but I sure loved how her face lit up with a smile as brilliant as the June sun.

The next day, we couldn't bypass a visit to Blarney Castle near Cork. Built over six hundred years ago by a renowned chieftain, Cormac McCarthy, myths, legends and tales surround this castle. It is said that if one climbs the 127 steps and kisses the Blarney Stone of Eloquence at the top, you'll never again be at a loss for words. Embracing all things Irish, I was determined to do it. As we exited the bus, the driver announced, "Everyone be back in the bus in one hour. Have a good time."

Climbing the steps was no small feat. The pathway alone to the castle was quite a hike. Some kind of force awakened in me at the start of the steep spiraling stairway. Most of the tour group had already gone up and some were even coming down. Without dawdling any further, I took a deep breath and started the slow, steady climb. The open air and bright sky at the top was refreshing. I took in deep breaths and thought I could almost touch a cloud as it drifted by. "Thank you, thank you, God." I murmured. As I peered down, I could see sheep looking like cotton balls dotting the hillside.

Mom wanted to kiss the stone first. It was tricky. She had to lie down on her back while bending backwards, hold tight to the guardrail on either side for safety while a man held onto her hips so she wouldn't fall. She kissed the stone with a big smack, plus another one just to be sure it took. "Bravo, Mom!" Then it was my turn. I did exactly the same thing. That kiss sent a zing through me from the top of my head to the bottom of my toes.

I took the steps down to ground level one at a time, backwards. Yes, backwards. They were so steep I'd have fallen on my face had I tried to go frontwards. Worried, scared, and greatly relieved at reaching the bottom, I retraced my steps on the long pathway to the bus, making it back just in the nick of time. I got a round of applause from my traveling companions. Some of them didn't believe I'd actually climbed to the top and kissed the famous stone, but I whipped out my souvenir picture as proof. Settling my weary bones down in my seat, great satisfaction filled me. Someday, I could tell this to my children.

I cherish my memories of this first trip abroad with Mom. I'm proud we belong to a heritage of people rich in history who fought for what they believed in, are deeply rooted in faith and who love music and family.

BACK AT HOME, my heart hammered hard when I read an advertisement in the local newspaper for Gresham Driving Aids. I never knew such devices existed. I didn't waste any time calling the owner, who had become a paraplegic as the result of an accident. After I explained my poor leg reflexes, he assured me that driving with hand controls was a viable option. The only requirement was a car with automatic transmission.

When I thought about purchasing a car, I recalled fond memories of the small dependable Volkswagen Beetle, like the one I rode in with my Grandpa. I was thrilled when I called the dealership to learn that 1968 was the first year that Volkswagen offered the option of an automatic transmission. A long-awaited dream was finally being realized.

Within a week, I was a licensed driver and a proud owner of a dark green Volkswagen Beetle equipped with hand controls. I could hardly believe I was legally in the driver seat. I drove cautiously into the village and attended morning Mass, then took the back road home to practice starting and stopping smoothly. It was tricky mastering the hand controls, learning to apply the correct amount of pressure to avoid spinning wheels, jackrabbit take-offs, and abrupt stops. I eased onto gravel at Wylie Road, figuring that at this early hour there would be little or no traffic. I savored the new green growth in the countryside and the novel idea of independence and power stirring within me as fresh air blew through the open windows.

Everything was going smoothly until I sensed a prickling—something was amiss. Immediately after, I heard a commotion ahead. Reaching the crest of the steep hill, my eyes popped. Just beyond my windshield, a herd of Holstein cows was rambling along the roadway, their hooves clip-clopping and their tails swishing, moving this way and that down the hill.

In the midst of this disorder, without invitation, fear opened the front door and jumped into the passenger seat beside me with a gruesome grin, screaming like a maniac, "Look out! Look out!"

But the cows weren't my worst concern. Risking a glance in the rearview mirror, I saw an old pick-up truck spit gravel after braking hard to avoid smacking my bumper. I couldn't stop, or pull over or back up. I had to keep moving forward. It wasn't all that far to the bottom of the large hill, but it sure seemed like a hundred miles.

I continued onward, controlling the brakes while trying to avoid hitting a cow. The herd somehow managed to keep a distance just inches from my car on either side. My shoulder blades hunched tightly as my right hand clamped down on the steering wheel and my left hand shakily clutched the break control. I coasted the rest of the way.

"Dear Mother of God, help me." The words spilled from my lips as the inner questions pounded in my ears. Why me? Why did some of the simplest things have to be so hard and complicated for me? Anger rivaled with fear for control of my emotions.

My face grew red hot when I heard the unmistakable sound of hearty laughter. *This is not a laughing matter, Lord.*

My spine straightened when I saw my girlfriend's father, Farmer Glen, standing at the bottom of the hill guiding his lead cows with his walking stick through the gateway into the northwest pasture. He wouldn't think this was so funny if I injured one of his prize milkers.

Didn't he know I was scared out of my wits? Didn't he know I wasn't able to get my license like his daughter did at sixteen? I had to wait all these years before I could legally drive!

He had been my neighbor for many years, yet I had never known him to take his herd to this pasture by way of the road. He nodded his head in recognition while calling out a cheery, "Good morning! A beautiful day, don't you think?" as I finally passed him safely.

Grrr. Slowly accelerating to a normal speed, I passed the marsh near Uncle Mike's house as the pick-up truck behind me sped by with the owner honking his horn. He was off my tail at last. I drove over a smaller hill, turned, and stopped at the corner before proceeding home. I coaxed the car into the drive, shut off the ignition, and removed the key, breathing a big sigh of relief, realizing yet again that it's a dangerous world out there, polio or no polio.

Forever afterwards, I remembered that as the "holy cow" practice drive. It took several years before I could laugh at the escapade. But I knew that practice makes perfect, so the next day, I was back on the road doing just that. I did, however, avoid the back road and early morning practice sessions.

A SOMBER, unfathomable sorrow struck right on the heels of the bizarre bovine incident. This growing-up episode struck me like a tornado and filled the family with fear. Our husky twenty-four-year-old Mike was suddenly troubled with severe headaches. The doctor informed us that he had an inoperable, aggressive brain tumor. Mike was hospitalized in critical care, never to walk or talk again. The raw cutting truth collapsed on us as if the roof had caved in. Mike was a wonderful father, devoted to his preschool sons and loving wife, and he was dying rapidly before our eyes.

Dad quickly verged on collapse. Overnight, he had the vitality of a bundle of dried cornstalks. Charlie, who was on active duty in the army, was called home from the war raging in Vietnam. Everyone was desperately out of kilter, feeling numb, heartbroken, and helpless.

We needed help. It was tearing me apart to see so much pain all around me. I had to find my center point and find Jesus, the source of my sustenance. I learned to trust Him, even when I felt myself sinking deeper and deeper into fear and defeat. Stepping out in faith, I found solace in the quiet of the hospital chapel. I poured out my crushing anguish

141

and helplessness and prayed for God's power to be unleashed to help us grow through this.

While praying, I heard an inner voice say, *Call Father Minck at the PIME Mission Seminary.* The last thing Father Minck had said to me after graduation was, "If you ever need anything, just give me a call." I called my priest friend. In wrenching sobs, I told him of our family crisis. He prayed with me over the phone, and without hesitation said, "I'm on my way."

After that prayer time and phone call, I knew God would give us the courage and strength to bear the unbearable. He was with us. Drying my tears, I went to Mike's room and was surprised to see no one else was present. Mike's strong, powerful chest was exposed and monitors were hooked up to his arms and upper body. His eyes were closed as he breathed heavily. He continued to appear agitated. Walking over, I took Mike's hand.

I was thankful for this moment to be alone with him, so I could open my heart to him. "If you can hear what I'm saying, then please squeeze my hand," I said.

He did!

"Can you blink your eyes too?"

He did!

"Praise God," I whispered. "Father Minck is coming, Mike. Hold on."

I told him what a great brother and father he was. I forgave him for scaring me with snakes and tormenting me during our early childhood. I asked his forgiveness for the times he felt robbed of Mom and Dad's attention because of all the fussing and care they gave me. I told him how proud Mom and Dad were of him and his sweet wife and sons. I thanked him for asking me to be godmother to his second son, Eddie. I promised to be good to the boys, and take them swimming and fishing at the lake. I told him I loved him and not to be afraid. "God is with us all, Mike. He's watching over us."

Mom opened the door and stepped inside. She told me that Bob would take me to the airport to pick up Father Minck. I gave Mike a kiss on the cheek, squeezed his hand, and said my last goodbye.

I do believe God brings people into our lives when they are needed. Father Minck was one of those people. He arrived in time to administer the Sacrament of the Last Rites, and he was with Mike when he drew his last breath. Father was a tremendous blessing and consolation. His celebration of Mike's life at the first White Mass of the Resurrection any of us had ever attended was beautiful.

The image of a loved one dying makes us all think about death. Throughout my childhood, I felt I would never live to adulthood because of the ravages of polio. But I did. And, ironically, my big, strong healthy brother died so very young. Barely two weeks after Mike's death, I began building a new life.

PRESIDENT JOHNSON AUTHORIZED the first federally funded Head Start Program in 1965, as an important part of the War on Poverty. It targeted low-income children who would be entering kindergarten in the fall, believing this support for school readiness gives children a stronger foundation as they enter kindergarten.

A recent graduate, in early June of 1968, I was hired to teach Dexter's summer Head Start Program and second grade in September. I was elated. While I would try to bolster kindergarteners' confidence, they would be bolstering mine. During the two-week training, I learned to appreciate how the Head Start curriculum was rich with opportunities to introduce literature, art, music, and nature study to children. Teaching children how to get along, how to be a friend, and promoting literacy activities with parents and their children was my job. I planned field trips to the police station and the fire department, and engaged speakers for various programs.

My first class had eighteen students. To my delight, we would meet at St. Joseph Catholic School in Dexter, the same school I had attended for eight years. As supplies were delivered, I started to establish a nurturing and safe environment where every child could thrive. I met with the cook to plan nutritious snacks and lunches. Before opening day, Sister Mary Patrick appeared at my door. "Well, Miss Ginger, you have everything shined and ready to go. Everything looks just great! Why, if I were one of your students, I'd love to have you for a teacher!"

"Just keep me and the class in your prayers," I said, smiling back at her, "Isn't it remarkable that I've come all the way back to my roots? God sure works in mysterious ways."

Walking to the sturdy old wooden teacher's desk, she pulled open the large bottom drawer, took out a worn and tarnished brass bell, gave it one last jingle, and placed it in my hands. "You do remember this, don't you?" When I felt the heft of that recess bell, my voice caught in my throat and my eyes misted. I felt her vote of confidence as she gave my hand another firm pat. I felt the authority pass from her to me.

With a sniff and a swipe at my eyes, I thanked this cherished teacher. "I'll treasure it."

"God bless you and all the children you will teach," Sister said. "And, don't ever forget that recess is important." We hugged, turned off the lights, and said our goodbyes.

At long last, I was a teacher.

THE ONE AND only time Dad visited my classroom was in the fall of 1968, during my first year of teaching second grade. My car needed servicing and Dad offered me a ride home.

At five-thirty, the halls were silent. Teachers had left for the day. I sat reflecting on the years of hard work and discipline required to get me here. With satisfaction, I surveyed the colorful art center, the cozy reading nook and the nature and science area I hoped would inspire the imaginations of the little ones.

My thoughts were interrupted when I heard Dad laughing and talking to old George, the janitor who was escorting him to my room. I started to pack.

"Take your time, there's no rush," Dad said.

I sat back down at the desk, rustled some papers and then pushed my internal pause button to linger on this once-in-a-lifetime moment. I watched Dad peruse the classroom in a wonderful silence. He slowly studied the informative bulletin boards, colorful displays, and children's projects and works. When he stopped in the nature corner of the room, it seemed like a benediction.

A bemused expression lit up his face and a chuckle escaped when he saw the small collection of animal homes. Hanging in a nook close to the ceiling was a large paper wasp nest attached to the branch of an oak tree. Dominic had brought this treasure from the woods to me. Various types of birds' nests grabbed Dad's attention—a well-preserved grass-lined robin nest, a tightly woven blue-gray gnatcatcher nest made from spider webs, down, lichen and bits of plant material, and a long Baltimore oriole nest. Puffy butterfly cocoons were affixed to the curtain by the window, waiting to hatch.

I thought of how Dad had taught me about all kinds of

animals and their architecture. When I was a little girl, his voice seemed tinged with magic when he spoke about animals' secrets and revealed their subtle details and marvelous beauty.

Continuing to make his way around the nature section, Dad fingered the long pheasant and the short blue-jay feathers, the deer antlers, the turtle shell, seashells, Petoskey stones, and smooth river-washed stones. He laughed when he examined one of the giant redwood pinecones that a student had brought from California. He'd never seen one of those before.

While I sat watching Dad in my classroom, it felt like watching a bear savoring honey from a honey tree. He reverently paged through a textbook, before he looked up with a sparkle in his eyes and a wide grin. "Okay, Teach, we better get going."

With that remark, I felt I had finally received his blessing on my chosen career.

13

SAFE, EFFECTIVE AND POTENT

DURING THE FOLLOWING CHRISTMAS HOLIDAY, I fell wildly and ecstatically in love. It turned out to be almost a ten-year long love affair with a virile, strong, energetic, fun-loving and devoted significant other introduced to me by my father, of all people. We were together as often as possible. He had a direct way of holding my eyes, like a magnet, with his dark brown eyes even if we were on the other side of a room from each other. He listened with such understanding and could sense my every need. I couldn't get enough of him, and he couldn't get enough of me. He was both a protector and friend. Duke filled a void like no other. My devoted German shepherd named Duke.

A Christmas surprise from Dad, my puppy was a lively fur ball with big paws. Duke captured my heart right from the start. We took short walks, went swimming, and loved going out in the boat. Taking responsibility for him and successfully raising him from a pup increased my confidence. I learned that I could provide and take care of not only myself, but another.

DURING MY FIRST semester of teaching, I became part of a national trend in schools, integrating borderline special-needs students into regular classrooms. I discovered a keen interest in learning more about how to work with this population of students. God, in His infinite wisdom, was using me as a vehicle for helping both the regular and the emotionally disturbed students. But not everyone thought like I did. Several teachers felt a basic fear because they were not trained to teach these students, who could be disruptive.

Growing up is a challenge no matter your background and circumstances. Some youngsters experience divorce, death, sickness, economic problems, and frequent moves. Any number of difficulties and emotional stresses play a big part. I wanted to be better equipped to help all the children I taught, and the best way I knew to do that pointed to graduate school. I didn't want to let time just drift by and keep stalling. Besides, I loved the stimulation of the university environment.

As an undergraduate, I had successfully managed a full session of summer school on the campus of Eastern Michigan University. The dorm, cafeteria, library, and classrooms were close to each other and accessible. I also considered finagling a way to earn my Masters degree at the University of Michigan, which offered a highly recommended program in special education.

I overrode the negative drone of buzzing thoughts and questions. *Are you crazy? You'll never be accepted. You'll be too tired to drive and attend evening classes after teaching all day. Where are you going to park? There might be great distances to walk to get to class. You don't even know if you can get into the buildings. What business do you have roaming around in the dark? It's not safe. Peculiar people lurk around that campus. Why put yourself in jeopardy?*

I submitted my application anyway.

When he was a three-year-old, Charlie called me "Ginky" instead of Ginger. Brother Dick picked up on this and has teased me with it ever since. Upon hearing about my acceptance to graduate school at U of M, he kidded me again. "Congratulations! You keep this up and someday I'll be calling you Dr. Ginky!"

I had been taught to aim high. I'd never know if I could accomplish something if I never tried. My family held the U of M in high esteem for its academic and athletic status, but they had misgivings about my navigation and safety on campus. I did too.

As I pulled my VW Bug into a tight parking space close to my building on the first day of classes, I felt like pinching myself to see if I was dreaming. Thrust into this alien environment with a mixture of people, philosophies, and religions, it took me quite a while to become comfortable with the beehive of activity all around campus. The huge first class I walked into, caused me to gulp and take the first empty seat.

My classes were held in the School of Education and in the Literature, Science and Arts buildings, where Pewabic tiles embellished the interiors with rich turquoise and lapis colors. My heart skipped a beat the day I discovered a plaque inside the Rackham Graduate Building commemorating the history-making event of April 12, 1955, when Dr. Thomas Francis of the University of Michigan School of Public Health announced the success of the Salk polio vaccine. "The vaccine works...It is safe, effective, and potent." After reading that plaque, I felt convinced that on this campus I, too, would be safe, effective, and potent.

How special it was for me to realize as an adult that this life-saving proclamation was announced to the world from the campus where I was a student. It made me all the more grateful that I, along with many other polio patients, had been rehabilitated by outstanding doctors trained at this great institution, despite some of the excruciating, humiliating, and embarrassing circumstances.

Although there was no such thing as handicapped parking in those days, I used small parking spots that accommodated my VW Bug. By means of railings at entrance steps and elevators, I was able to access these buildings. Luckily, by the next fall session when I had a late class, Duke was well-trained to walk with me on his leash. He was an enormous help. After a full day of teaching, I found his gentle pull helped me along on my way to classes so my body didn't have to work so hard. He would sit quietly next to me during class. I had no fear whatsoever about walking back to my car in the dark and driving home with Super Dog as a companion.

I had the pleasure of studying under Dr. William Morse, renowned in the field of special education, who was as welcoming to Duke as to me. He was witty, wise, and knowledgeable, with extensive experience working in the field. It surprised me to learn that for many years he and his family lived on the property of the Fresh Air Camp at Patterson Lake, the polio camp I attended during my girlhood. He was instrumental in converting this facility to serve the special education population when polio swiftly became eradicated after the vaccine. This was my favorite class because of Dr. Morse's excellent teaching and mentoring, as well as our mutual love of the camp.

In the final summer before I obtained my Master of Arts degree in special education, I was delighted to receive a fellowship to teach for eight weeks at the U of M Hospital School, where I had been taught as a patient. This was the last summer before the school was transferred to the new Mott Children's Hospital.

The old school was just as I remembered. Dean Lidgard, the principal, was encouraging. He started me with a special assignment. I donned a surgical gown and mask to visit with a seven-year-old who had been severely burned when he emptied the trash into a barrel and lit the debris. An aerosol can had ignited and enveloped him in flames. He was flown to our hospital from Canada, swathed from head to toe in bandages, bedridden and almost completely immobile. My heart ached when I looked into his dark eyes. Apart from his mouth, they were the only visible part of his anatomy.

Without flinching, I looked directly into those eyes and in a soft, loving voice told him my name, a little bit about myself, and yes, I was a real person behind the silly outfit. I was happy to come in for a short visit.

"Bonjour, mon ami," he said in a weak voice.

Thanks to my three years of French classes, we were able to exchange a few phrases in the twenty to thirty minutes I was permitted. I shared a French story and song.

I visited him twice that week. The nurse said it helped lighten his agitation. When I took my undergrad French classes, little did I know that they would benefit a very young and precious life. This unique experience in a sterile, hospital environment taught me we all have something to give and share with one another, no matter how small or insignificant, or how long the time.

Shortly after meeting the little boy, I felt a seismic shift in my inner core when I learned that my new little friend had died. My only comfort was that I helped to make his last days a little lighter. I'm grateful my faith helped me through the following days and weeks. I've never forgotten this child. He taught me reverence for each and every day, and appreciation for each person I meet. He also reminded me of the stone-cold fact that little people die, even in an exceptional hospital. I remembered my childhood roommate, Blossom, once again.

His death helped equip me for a sadness that came months later in the fall. One of my pupils contracted the flu and died a week later of Reye's Syndrome. His family, classmates, and community were devastated. I had the responsibility of helping his classmates learn a hard lesson about death.

Starting classes for an advanced degree early in my career proved to be the right decision for me. After attending evening classes during fall and spring sessions and shouldering heavier loads in summer sessions for three years, I proudly received my Master of Arts degree in special education from the University of Michigan. Dick has called me "Dr. Ginky" ever since.

ON A COLD SUNDAY morning after church services in March of 1971, I sat on a small wooden bench in front of an old vacated fisherman's house on Portage Lake in Pinckney, Michigan, near my childhood stomping grounds. A sacred solitude surrounded me, and I felt a profound sense of gratitude for finding this place.

It was always my dream to own a lakefront home. I wondered if my recent offer to purchase this particular piece of property on a land contract would ever be realized. The lake is the finest all-sports freshwater in the area. I whispered a prayer for the Lord to give me a sign that my efforts were not in vain. The sun shone on some letters traced on the dirty, dusty attic window. I spelled the letters out loud as I tried to make them out. J. E. S. U. S. Graffiti of one kind or another can usually be found on an abandoned building, yet nothing else was disturbed. This sign filled me with an assurance that God's hand was blessing my endeavor.

In July, I took ownership on the same weekend that my niece Kelly had her seventh birthday. Both commemorative events were celebrated with a family party at the lake, since the temperature was in the nineties. This was the first of many family summer gatherings there.

After the parties, the first major work on the property was to clear the land of dry-rotted fishing boats, remove three mature willow trees that loomed over the roof and also dispose of the broken and unsafe sidewalk that ran from the kitchen door to the lake. Jerry undertook a big chunk of this job. Dominic and Paul, who were familiar with concrete work, decided that the rickety seawall should also be replaced. The sidewalk and carport turned out well, and the boys poured a seawall that was the envy of the neighborhood. The repairs continued. Heating and electrical systems were eventually replaced, an upstairs addition constructed and a new roof installed.

The next thing I did was to try to figure out what to do with an odd window on the side of the house in the front room. It was 60 inches high and 18 inches wide. I wanted the light to come in, but still wanted privacy. I pictured a dove, representing the Holy Spirit, flying over a body of water with golden rays on the top and the bottom. I presented my sketch to an artist and had it made into a stained-glass window. This was my blessing window, completed and set in place just before the Thanksgiving holiday.

It didn't take long to acquire three boats to take full advantage of living life on the waterfront. The first boat was an aluminum canoe I named "Glider," which we used when the lake was like glass. The second was a Super Porpoise, a red-hulled sailboat with a red and white stripe sail that I named "Skimmer." I used this boat when the wind was up.

The third was a small pontoon boat that I christened "Cruiser," useful most anytime, accommodating a party of friends or family.

At this time in my life, I could pedal a special bike. I first saw the adult-sized three-wheelers with a big basket in Florida where they were popular. It exercised my legs. I didn't have to worry about losing balance, and I could pedal on the level private roads in the neighborhood. Duke was always eager to tag along. It was good exercise for him too. My young niece, Nikki, who lived on a nearby side street, would wave and run along beside us if she was out playing in her yard.

I knew that my education had paid off, helping me achieve my goal of home ownership. I reflected on the many times I sat in the offices of doctors and stared at their diplomas prominently displayed. I remembered thinking that since I had my own place, I would pull out my four sheepskins that were buried in a file cabinet and hang them in a work study corner. My St. Joseph School 8th grade diploma, St. Thomas High School diploma, Madonna College Bachelor of Arts diploma, and University of Michigan Master of Arts diploma would have a meaningful place. They were symbols of monumental effort, testimonies of faith, and a reminder to stay the course and to achieve goals.

During the first decade of my teaching, the Dexter Jaycees honored me at a special banquet as their choice to receive the Outstanding Young Educator Award. Dad and Mom were my guests. I was so pleased, especially that Dad agreed to go, dressed in his best suit. Dad seldom gave verbal praise. The fact that he attended was a statement in itself. Before long, that plaque took center place on the wall with my diplomas.

AT THE DOCTOR'S OFFICE, something that felt like an unexpected blizzard swirled in my head, freezing the pipes in my throat and the blood in my veins, as surely as an arctic blast might freeze the gasoline line of a car or water pipes of a home. Mom and I were here to receive vaccinations before our trip to Mexico City, Guadalajara, and Acapulco in the spring of 1971. Mom was fifty-seven years young, and I was twenty-five years old. Learning that one injection was for polio alarmed me. I protested.

"You're putting yourself in jeopardy by refusing the recommended polio vaccine, young lady," said the doctor. "You'll be passing through some questionable territory."

Mom stuck out her chin, rolled up her sleeve, like in the picture of the brave Rosie the Riveter, and stepped forward to receive her injections. "Don't you remember that you and your brothers and sisters were inoculated shortly after the polio vaccine came out in 1956? You didn't have any after-effects then, and you won't now. You can do it."

The doctor swabbed Mom's arm, adding, "This vaccine will protect you. There are three strains of polio. It is possible for you to be re-infected if you're exposed to a wild virus." Despite the World Health Organization and Rotary International's continual fight to eradicate this horrendous disease, its variations still pop up in some corners of our world.

I wanted to curl up into a tight ball, taking the hedgehog approach, and disengage. Yet when I'm in, I'm all in. I had committed to this trip. I closed my eyes, prayed, held out my arm, and received the shot. Mom was the best person to teach me to grow wings and fly. She believed in celebrating what works and doing what needs to be done when it needs to be done.

Traveling together with the most beloved person in my life was an honor. To soar over the border into Mexico City and the University of Mexico put us into a totally different environment that awakened our senses with an explosion, starting with the hub-bub of the sound of Spanish and mariachi music that we heard in the shops and streets. We were fascinated by the sight of massive islands of street flowers, the colorful clothing worn by the people, and the iconic murals, sculptures and paintings

I was intrigued with Diego Rivera and especially his talented wife, Frida Kahlo. She contracted polio at the age of six. She survived with a damaged right leg and foot and walked with a limp. In early adulthood, she severely injured her hip, pelvis, and spine in a bus accident. During a long recovery, she learned to paint, depicting some of her physical challenges in graphic details. Her story inspired me. We drank in the vibrant city, rich with history, inspiring art, and friendly people.

We looked forward to our visit to the celebrated Shrine of Our Lady of Guadalupe, Patroness of the Americas, located outside of Mexico City. On December 9, 1531, Juan Diego, a fifty-seven-year-old convert to the faith, was climbing over the top of Tepeyac Hill on his way to morning Mass when Mary, the Mother of Jesus, appeared to him dressed in native garb. She asked him to pick the roses that were growing out of season, carry them inside his cloak, and present them to the Bishop as a sign to carry out her request to build a shrine in this place, so she could demonstrate her love, her protection, and her compassion for the people. He obeyed. When he presented the roses and her request to the Bishop, Mary's image appeared on his woven cloak made from the fibers of the Maguey cactus.

Reaching the grounds, we saw pilgrims praying while crawling on their knees to the entrance of the Basilica. When I was twelve years old, I had seen this same devotion practiced at the Shrine of St. Anne De Beaupre in Quebec as a way for people to honor God with their bodies while humbling their hearts in worshiping on holy ground.

Thousands of miracles have occurred there over the years. Here in this place, as in Quebec, the walls near a side entrance are lined with braces, crutches, and canes left as wordless testimony by those who were physically healed.

I had so often dreamed of being normal—able to run and dance, and be free of assistive devices and free of pain. In spite of years of surgeries and rehabilitation, I wasn't healed. But God could cure me. I'd wanted to unstrap my brace and hang it up in this place and waltz out of here as a whole person. It would be a beautiful miracle.

As a preteen, after having surgery to correct my left drop foot by inserting large screws to hold it upright, I suffered with excruciating pain for two weeks straight. The heavy white cast was soon stained and saturated with reddish-brown blood. In spite of being elevated three pillows high, it still throbbed with endless, deep, deep pain. I can't count the number of times I tried my best to not scream for a pain shot before it was time to get another one. Screaming wouldn't do any good anyway. I still had to wait.

During this terrible, awful time, you better believe I asked Jesus for healing. I begged Him to take it all away and to be healed. I got a "no." He asked me to offer my suffering for the salvation of souls and the greater honor and glory of God. He promised the suffering would not be wasted, and He would always be with me. So, I gave my "yes" to God. Ever since this time, I've relied on His grace to steady and sustain me. I shared this with my mom at the shrine. I gained an understanding and peace about my resolution, knowing it would be the right answer either way.

Inside the Basilica, the authentic Sacred Image of Our Lady has remained intact for nearly five centuries, hanging in a place of honor behind the main altar. After hearing Holy Mass and gazing one last time at the image of Our

VIRGINIA FORD

Lady of Guadalupe, I felt the love of Mary fill me. It was as if she enfolded me in her mantel, wrapping me in a warm protective hug before I had to leave. On the way to the exit, an older peasant man, short in stature, approached me. Looking kindly into my eyes, he smiled and handed me a long-stemmed red rose before quietly walking away. I took this as a visible sign that Jesus and Mary loved me. Even though I wasn't healed, I left this place with a special sense of the Lord's blessing.

———

TEOTIHUACAN IS RENOWNED for the world's third-largest pyramid. The Pyramid of the Sun rises almost 210 feet high, with 248 steps to the top. The second notable pyramid is the Pyramid of the Moon, 150 feet high, but built on steeper ground. These two pyramids are said to harbor great mystical energy, so people come here to meditate. I had reservations about visiting this ancient city whose religion involved offering living sacrifices of animals and humans to their gods. Even the main road to the pyramids, called Avenue of the Dead, sounded foreboding and made me shiver.

The pyramids seemed even more impressive in size as tourists walked about the sprawling two-mile distance in this very harsh and desolate place under a blistering noonday sun. Mom and others climbed to the tops to see different perspectives. It was too much for me. I stayed below in the big empty wasteland amongst the ancient structures and took some pictures. After a while, I rested on a bench, contemplating the history of this strange, gloomy place.

My hands felt grimy after the long morning traipsing about the ruins in the scalding heat. As I hurried to use the restroom before boarding the bus, I was the only one in the facility. I set the camera down on the counter next to the washbasin, washed my hands thoroughly, turned to tear a paper towel from the dispenser, and dried my hands. Reaching over to pick up the camera, I blurted out, "What the heck? Where's my camera?" I checked the floor and searched around to no avail. I neither saw nor heard anyone. Stunned, I knew a thief had ripped me off. Hustling outside to look sharply in all directions, I saw no one in the vicinity except in the far-off distance where our group was boarding the bus.

Upon entering the bus, I slunk over to where mom was sitting, clamped myself to her side, put my head on her shoulder and cried. I couldn't help it. "What's the matter? Are you sick? Did something happen to you?"

I told her my woeful tale and that I felt sad and violated. It was a valuable Argus camera and meant a lot to me. My godfather had given it to me as a twelfth-grade graduation present. Also, the special memorable pictures from this trip had been stolen from me too.

She comforted me. "Well, don't fret, making yourself sick and letting it ruin your trip. No one can steal the memories from where it matters the most, right in here," as she patted me. "It's best to forgive the offender and let it go."

On our way to Acapulco, we passed through rough countryside where poor peasants dwelled. Living in hovels pieced together from found objects and substandard materials, gardening in poor soil with hand tools and perhaps a burro, raising goats and a few chickens, they strived to provide for their families. I didn't have to stretch my imagination much to believe that the wild polio virus might be lurking in some of these areas. And it also made me reconsider the loss of my camera. I had so much. They had nothing.

It was much easier to tolerate the sun and enjoy it when

we were able to cool off in the coastal breeze and swim in the refreshing water at the beach in Acapulco. At low tide, the wet sand packed down hard and smooth on the level shoreline. Discovering I could walk a good distance without my brace and knee buckling made me feel strong and healthy.

A pleasure cruise the next afternoon along the coastline offered much to see with all the beautiful homes, small parks and marinas. Water birds were active and playful dolphins swam alongside the boat seeming to be as curious as we were. We had two funny keepsake pictures of Mom and me taken when a surprise swashbuckling pirate appeared on deck with his fake—but real-looking—knife in his hand, and circulated among the guests. At least we could go home with two pictures to show for our Mexican trip.

Too soon, our trip came to an end. A short time before landing, a stewardess handed out custom forms to declare gifts purchased in Mexico. We had much more than monetary gifts to take home. Mom and I knew this would be our last big trip together for a number of reasons, but especially because of my Dad's health issues. It made me think of our previous trips together, expanding our love and appreciation of each other.

I also realized that despite having a family of eleven, Mom had given me more than my fair share of good times. These trips were special blessings, a way of saying, "Thank you" to Mom. They celebrated the end of my childhood struggling with polio and the long road of rehabilitation. As Mom began her retirement and I entered early adulthood, the holidays to foreign places helped us see where we came from and offered a peek ahead to where we might be going.

14

A SOLO TRIP TO GRAND BAHAMA

I HAD no indecision in planning the next vacation in the spring of 1974. I simply wanted a place with sunny, warm temperatures outside the USA. I wanted to prove to myself that I could travel independently.

More importantly, I had recently had a marriage proposal. He seemed to be a good man but he had a history. He was talented musically and was a whiz as a car mechanic. He owned a modest home and had a steady job. He was divorced, with no children and had an annulment. But I really only knew two of his friends and I knew none of his family. His parents were deceased and he had a sister who was not in his life very much. But he was active in the church and the three nuns I taught Sunday school with at St. Mary's Church in Pinckney liked him. My Mom and the brothers that knew him did not believe he was right for me, but left it at, "It's your decision." I think that I still had some thinking to do before saying "I do." I needed to escape.

I needed time to ask myself some serious questions. Why couldn't I say "yes?" Well I do know the answer—he really wasn't the one. An even bigger log in the road centered on my polio issues. I needed to come to terms with that fact. It was playing a big part in my decision to marry or to remain single. Hoping I could figure things out on this trip, I decided to go solo to the Grand Bahama Island.

I left feeling like I'd been hit by a thunderstorm that blocked my way with tangled tree limbs, clutter and debris. My only recourse was God. I had a strong urge to draw near to my Creator, to seek His will, to clarify my purpose and role in life, to recharge, to rest in His presence.

I attended Easter Sunday Mass in a chapel nestled on the bluff overlooking the sea, with about thirty local parishioners. The worship area was full of the scent of Easter lilies. At first, I felt odd being the only white person, but was back in my comfort zone with their warm, friendly reception. One pretty mother was nursing her baby and offered a "Happy Easter" as I sat in a pew across the aisle from her. A bunch of doll-like barefoot girls in white dresses with their hair in cornrows and huge white bows stole my heart. They had beautiful eyes, shy smiles, and pure angel voices. The overall reverence and soulful singing of the entire congregation, with their "Alleluias" going straight into heaven, almost resurrected me right out of the pew.

Upon leaving the chapel, I noticed the mother with the newborn was walking with a limp and wearing a leg brace. Her handsome husband at her side was holding the hand of their darling preschool son. I was grateful to God for bringing me to Grand Bahama Island to finally see, with my own eyes, a husband with his wife who was definitely a polio survivor, and their sweet children.

Back at my private spot at the end of the beach, I had soaked in all the island and the sea had to offer. Refreshed and renewed in mind, body and spirit, I had lots of time to think and prioritize my thoughts and feelings in this simple, lovely place. I was ready for business with God, ready to lay all my concerns and fears on the table and make some decisions concerning my future. Should I remain single, or marry?

Taking stock of myself, I knew I had successfully babysat for children from two-year-olds to ten-year-olds with no problems. I had accomplished much in my education and personal life. I loved my career. I tested my mettle in becoming a homeowner, keeping house, and managing my finances. I had successfully raised and trained Duke, contributed to my parish in teaching religious studies, and I sang in the choir. I loved all my family, including twenty-plus nieces and nephews and had enjoyed adventures with them in waterfront activities, arts and crafts, and encouraging them along in their lives' journeys. These were all blessings, I reminded myself.

My concerns boiled down to accepting the facts and believing that I could be loved and cherished as a wife and become a mother of healthy, happy children, despite my polio disabilities. Would I be bedridden for six months? How could I manage with all that extra weight with my legs and back? How could I manage caring for a newborn?

Then I remembered Mom frequently saying, "God makes the back to fit the burdens of life. He'll never give you more than you can carry." It stuck in my mind in regard to the ability to bear children and especially, to care for them the first year when they couldn't walk.

All of this baby business was very difficult for me to imagine going through when I was surrounded by physically healthy women, several of whom had experienced difficult pregnancies in spite of not having a serious disease like polio. I had never met a woman with paralytic polio like myself who had successfully borne children of her own. The U of M Hospital was like a second home to me. I'd worked in Saint Joseph Mercy Hospital. I'd traveled. I wasn't blind. I thought I should have seen at least a few.

The closest I'd ever come to knowing polio mothers were women from my home church. One had a withered arm. The other had a weak leg—but no braces and she walked with only a slight limp. Both had healthy children, and as friends they encouraged me and offered their prayers for me. "You're not one to run from life," they said. "Leave the children thing up to God. Take it one step at a time. If you marry and have children, you're doubly blessed. There's no guarantee for anybody, but you can sure have fun trying!"

Medically, my doctors assured me that in all likelihood, I could conceive and have children. In all probability, I'd need to slow down in the last three months, to do more sitting and keep my feet elevated. I could do that. It all came down to hard core faith. I believed in the sacred union of marriage as a sacrament that gives grace. The single life had its merits, but I did desire to marry. God had put that desire for marriage and children in my heart. I knew that. Life is not always easy. There on that island, I saw the light. I put my trust in God.

Yes, then and there, I decided I would marry, but I would not marry Mr. Wrong. I would not settle. Polio or not, I believed God would provide the right husband for me.

On my last visit to the beach, God told me loud and clear, "BE NOT AFRAID." So I decided to leave Satan's lies and negativity there, to dry them out in the sun and let them drift away with the tide.

15

THE CHARISMATIC MOVEMENT

IN THE LATER part of the 1970s I became interested in the Charismatic Renewal in the Roman Catholic Church. A major hub of this renewal was located in Ann Arbor. This ecumenical group known as the Word of God was fully endorsed by my spiritual advisor and friend, Father Minck, who for a number of years had nudged me to participate.

Father Minck asked me to host two religious sisters from India who were connected with the PIME Missions. I agreed. They were visiting the States for mission appeals and desired to learn about the renewal in our area between their speaking engagements. I not only provided transportation, but attended a major conference, prayer meetings, and social events with Sister Bethina and Mother Celestine.

As a novice, Sister Bethina had studied in New York and became fluent in English. Years later, she became the Assistant General of her order, the Catechist Sisters of St. Ann. Although mainly a teaching order, it also served the poor in orphanages and hospitals.

Sister Bethina was seven years my senior, petite, and

dynamic. Our whole family came to love her zest for living and her deep faith. She offered small gifts in thanksgiving for our hospitality—a wooden, hand-carved letter opener, a sandalwood necklace and a silk sari. Yet her best gift was the gift of herself. As she showed us how to put the sari on, sing the songs and chants and dance the dances of the Indian culture, she brought a ray of warmth and beauty into our home.

Since she had never been around large bodies of water, learning to swim was both a desire and a challenge. And a great source of amusement. Dressed in one of my bathing suits and an oversized T-shirt, she took swimming lessons every day and learned to float on her back, tread water, dog paddle, and blow bubbles.

Eyeing the sailboat one windy day, Sister Bethina was willing to accept my brother-in-law's invitation to go for a ride. Feeling brave in her bright orange life vest, she boarded the boat for a zippy sail. When she got back on land, she said, "I prayed to Jesus for protection, thanked him for this lake, and couldn't stop laughing."

Before the end of August, when the sisters had to return to India, the prayers of Father Minck and these nuns helped my spirit to ignite and I embraced the renewal movement. So did my mother and brother Jerry. The biggest draw for me was the positive commitment and dignity toward marriage and family life that I saw over and over again. I was getting closer to wanting marriage and saw it as a viable option, especially after witnessing many of the wonderful marriages in the charismatic movement.

In October of 1977, we received the distressing news that our beloved missionary priest, Father Minck, was diagnosed with an aggressive and terminal cancer and was given about six months to live. That winter we lived under the umbrella of death. At Christmas, I gave him a brown and tan afghan I'd crocheted to help keep him warmer and more comfortable during his sickness. Although he rapidly became frail, he was strong in spirit. By March he was unable to communicate with us. Any day we expected to hear of his death.

But death visited us closer to home first.

On March 28, 1978, Dad left home for good without even so much as a "goodbye." On this final exit, he left everyone and everything behind. He was rushed to the hospital and died of congestive heart failure at six months shy of his sixty-eighth birthday. We had all seen his health plummet after his retirement, but we were not prepared for his sudden death.

As I stood in the doorway of my parents' bedroom, hesitant to enter, I sighed heavily and slumped to one side. The soft glow of the lamp spotlighted Dad's wallet, key ring, rosary, pocketknife, and loose change on top of the dresser—items he'd never leave behind when he left home.

I stared at the tan wallet. Curiosity drew me over to check it out. It looked worn and tired, lumpy, not classy or sophisticated. It didn't zip closed or snap together. It was a simple flip wallet. I remember some of the times when he opened it, to turn most of his earnings over to Mom for groceries, to pay the bills, reserving money to fill the car with gas, to put money in the collection basket at church, to pay the barber for his monthly haircut, an allotment of Camel cigarettes and maybe a six-pack of Stroh's for the weekend, especially during the hot summer.

Taking the wallet in hand, I flopped on the bed, opened it and secretly hoped it would somehow put me in touch with Dad. The expected things appeared front and center— his Social Security and Blue Cross/Blue Shield cards. But then my fingers felt a square of felt. I pulled a brown scapular from an insert pocket and a plastic-covered picture of the Sacred Heart of Jesus, along with a silver dollar with Lady Liberty on the front. Appearing next was his driver's license listing his height, weight, color of hair and eyes. Those eyes, with a hint of a smile, looked directly out at me. The bittersweet taste of salty tears streamed into the corners of my mouth as I swiped them away.

Dad said, *"Hi, there, Ginger Girl. No more tears."*

I do believe I saw him wink!

I sat straight up and thumbed through another fold in the wallet. A sliver of light pierced my darkness as I found a 2x2-inch brown sienna engagement photo of twenty-two-year-old, handsome Dad in a snazzy dress suit with one arm around lovely Mom, wearing a tailored suit, fur boa, and hat that framed her happy face.

Reaching inside the deepest pocket, I extracted a flattened wad of graduation pictures of his eleven children and a group picture of his grandchildren. Next came a yellowed newspaper clipping of his brother Frank, with commentary about his career in the army. The last item was a newspaper article about my Teacher of the Year Award.

A little more than a week after Dad's burial, Father Minck died. Mom and I attended his funeral at the PIME mission house. As he lay in state at his Mass of the Resurrection dressed in his white priestly vestments and holding his gold chalice, he looked serene and peaceful. Neither Mom nor I had ever attended a funeral for a priest before. Having known the man and his mission, we found it an honor and a privilege.

After returning home, we resumed our lives knowing that both Father Minck and my own earthly father would now be with us only in spirit. Both were great men who played major roles in my life.

ONE SATURDAY in the springtime of 1980 I was invited to a dinner party, where I was formally introduced to the hosts' friend, Eric Ford. They had encouraged Eric to come to Ann Arbor from Ohio to be part of the renewal. Before long, he purchased a home in the northwest part of the city. As a single man, he was their frequent guest for Saturday dinners. We had previously caught each other's eye at various gatherings, service projects and prayer meetings, but had never spoken to each other.

Before dinner, the couple's two-year old crawled onto Eric's knee with a book in her hand. He didn't shoo her away, but rather settled her comfortably up in the crook of his arm. She gave a little sigh, and in seconds her thumb was in her mouth as she contentedly listened to the story.

After dinner, while I was helping with dishes, their eight-year-old son approached Eric and asked if he wanted to shoot some baskets before dark. Eric didn't hesitate to agree. As I gazed out the window, it was hard to tell who was having more fun, the young boy or Eric. The adults talked, shared stories, and played cards while the children were put to bed. I got to know Eric a little better and liked how naturally he acted around children. Strangely, the thought of envisioning him as a father was easy and somehow very appealing.

Eric had a dimension and complexity to his character that made me curious enough to want to know him better, so I invited him to a singles' party out at the lake. My brother Jerry knew I was interested, so he planned to give this guy a little initiation to see how he'd react. Eric didn't waterski, but he was game for going tubing. Jerry drove the boat as fast as he could go, and hit every big wave that he encountered head on. Eric held tight and didn't let go. Back on shore, Eric looked him straight in the eye, laughed heartily, and said, "Well, that was quite a ride."

During the next two years, I had numerous opportunities to see the different sides of Eric especially after I asked him out for our first official date. I was given

tickets to the Dexter Community Theater production of
Oklahoma with the Dexter Community Orchestra providing
the music, and I invited Eric along. I thought it would be a
great first date. Who doesn't like musicals?

At this time in my career, I was teaching first grade in
the historic Copeland Building that was actually the first
high school in Dexter where my mom went to high school.
It was serving kindergarten and first grade classes while the
new Cornerstone K-2nd grade school was being built. The
community used its gym with a full stage for plays. Eric
and I went through the front doors, turned right and
peeked into my classroom before entering the gym for the
play. He was pleasantly surprised. He got to admire my
students' work in the hallway and in the class cabinets. He
also got to be introduced to—as he tells the story—half the
town of Dexter before taking his seat, and more during
intermission, and afterwards as well when he met folks
from the band and some of the actors that I knew.

This turned out to be a hit date. Eric opened up about a
whole side of himself I never knew. That night I learned
that he loved many of the Broadway musicals and played
their music on the piano. Although his Mom was the one to
encourage him to play the piano starting when he was a
youngster, his Dad sang these songs passionately and
inspired Eric all the more. Eric learned a little more about
me and my hometown background on this date as well.

Another date was kind of spur of the moment. Both our
jobs had kept us very busy one week. Eric called and was
able to get away late, straight from work saying, "Let's at
least go for salad and good pizza some place local." At this
time in my area, that meant the Dam Site Inn in the town of
Hell. Although a favorite eatery of the motorcycle crowd,
they served the best pizza around.

We went in and were looking for an empty table when I
heard a voice call out, "Well, lookie here." My brother

Dominic said, "Come on over and have a seat." Eric helped me off with my coat and pulled a chair out for me, tucking the coat behind me. He in turn, unbuttoned his trench coat, put it over the back of his chair and started to sit down when Dominic spouted, "Hold on. "What the heck are you wearing a tie for?" He stood and started to yank on it saying, "Take that thing off and loosen up a little. I can't have you sitting at my table with that thing on. It's embarrassing."

"Well, alright, if you insist," Eric replied chuckling and throwing me a quizzical look.

"Eric, let me introduce you to my brother Dominic," I said, laughing.

One by one, Eric met most of my siblings. I think he was fascinated by my large family. He thought he came from a big one with five children. Well, he received a little education when he finally met all of mine, especially when they were all together. He got this chance at my youngest brother Paul's wedding in Wisconsin when I invited him as my guest. I knew that he needed to see what he was getting himself into if he was serious about marrying me.

My oldest sister Frankie and her husband Jerry invited Eric and me to take the road trip with them as the back seat of their van was empty. We had a fine time. The sisters all approved of him. Frankie got to check Eric out and she had only good things to say about him. Actually, everyone liked him, but for some reason each one of the boys had to have some fun with him at his expense. What is it with brothers? Here at this wedding he heard other stories of the brothers and their initiations and he managed to survive a little more easily when he heard about how they first taunted my brothers-in-law.

When Eric was in a ratty t-shirt and jeans with holes, wore his baseball cap backwards, and sweated bullets while engrossed in yard work, I found him very sexy. I also loved the way he looked when cleaned up, wearing a crisp shirt, suit, and tie. He carried himself well with his broad shoulders and refined manners, and he smelled wonderfully of Bay Rum cologne. He sent my senses rocketing. His acceptance of all of me quieted and dispelled any doubts I had. The trust I felt with him helped me to believe that I could be a lover, a wife, and possibly a mother to his children.

ON THE EVENING of March 16th in 1983, I set the gauge of the electric blanket on my bed to medium, drank a cup of hot chocolate, turned the heat down and the lights off and hopped into my warm cozy nest at ten o'clock. I set the alarm for 6:30 a.m. I listened to the moaning wind outside while saying some night prayers, and soon fell asleep.

Buzzz-z-z-z. "Somebody's at the door, Grandma," I said out loud in a surprised voice.

"Go answer it," she said smiling mischievously.

The buzzing continued as I slowly began awakening to reality. I didn't want to wake up.

It seemed I was on the cusp of something delightful and monumental. I was cocooned in a lovely gauzy material, yet felt like I was on the verge of breaking out into the warm sunshine.

Sitting up, I realized I had dreamed of Grandma! We were in her living room drinking hot tea and watching her favorite soaps—*Search for Tomorrow, As the World Turns* and *The Guiding Light*. Oh, how my Grandma loved drama, especially when it came to love stories. It was as if she were right here now, only that couldn't be true. She'd been dead for years, and I was now an adult living on my own, and had done so for a good long time. What a dream. It was so real, I had goose bumps! I wondered what brought that on.

Rubbing the sleep from my eyes, I remembered it was St. Patrick's Day. I'd better wear my warm green sweater and plaid wool skirt today to the classroom, I decided. My first grade students were in for a fun day at school. Eric would be taking me out afterwards for corned beef and cabbage. Grandma would approve, knowing that St. Patrick's Day was a great time for people to come together. This last holiday of winter held the promise of spring and new beginnings. I decided that Grandma would like Eric, too. I greeted her out loud. "Top o' the morning, Grandma."

On the way into work, the sun did its best to shine through the thickening clouds until a light snow began to fall. After dinner that night, the snow was deep and continued to fall heavily. Eric dropped me off with a hurried goodbye. The roads were getting worse by the minute, and he had a twenty-mile trip back to Ann Arbor.

Looking out the window, I saw the wind whipping the trees, shaking their arthritic limbs menacingly. The day had turned from a mild morning to a wild evening. No doubt, if this kept up, there'd be no school tomorrow. I whispered a prayer for Eric's safety, dimmed the lights, started a fire in the fireplace, and sat down to read. About an hour passed before the doorbell rang. I figured it was my brother Dominic, who lived nearby, checking on me to see if everything was all right.

Turning on the porch light, I sensed Grandma affectionately watching over me. My eyes opened wide in befuddlement and my nerves started to jangle like wind chimes when I answered and saw Eric standing there. A grin slowly emerged, tilting his mouth in an attractive daredevilish kind of way. He looked disheveled. His smiling face warmed me as he said, "I guarantee you're not going to work tomorrow. School will be canceled."

"Are you okay?"

"Well, I am, but I blew two tires when I hit a bad patch

of potholes on the road in front of your Grandma's driveway. I drove at a snail's pace into Dexter and parked at the gas station, which of course is closed. The only thing open was the Pub. I spotted your brother Paul as he was leaving. He dropped me off here."

He asked to borrow my spare tire to get him back To Ann Arbor. "I'll hook back up with Paul when the roads are clear," he promised, adding, "but it won't be tonight. Can I bunk on your couch?"

"Get in here and close the door," I said, kissing him tenderly on the cheek. "I guess since Grandma whammed you, stopping you right in your tracks, I'm obligated to have you stay."

"Your Grandma? What has she got to do with this?"

I giggled as we settled in front of the hearth and bundled under some quilts to keep warm. I heard Grandma whisper, "I'm not going to let this time pass without helping you make a commitment. Every path in life has a few potholes, my dear. Tonight, my prayer is that you both see the road rise clear before you."

That evening we talked seriously about our relationship. By the end of the month we were officially engaged. Every St. Patrick's Day since then, I raise a toast to Grandma.

Three components convinced me Eric was the one I had been waiting for—his deep faith in Jesus as his Lord and Savior, our ability to communicate, and that when we exchanged our wedding vows to each other, we each meant, "I do, for life."

On June 24, 1983, we said our vows. For two years we had held each other's hands. It was now time to hold each other's hearts.

We were married on a lovely summer evening in my hometown historical church of St. Joseph. Donna made my veil, mid-waist in length and bordered with lace flowers. My floor-length gown featured an empire waist with long sleeves and a high neckline with an inset of lace and pearls. I wore T-strap shoes with a steel shank that attached to the leg brace. These shoes were only worn for special occasions, and this time they were dyed white. I carried a cascade of white and pink sweetheart roses, stephanotis, ivy and baby's breath. A pearl rosary was interwoven in the bouquet.

I regarded Nell as my best friend in the Word of God. We were both single and we shared many good times together. And she and her boyfriend spent time with Eric and me. She too, came from a big family, loved to swim and play the guitar, and was spirit-filled. It was fitting that I chose her as my maid of honor.

Eric and his best man Jerry, a good friend and neighbor from Ann Arbor, were handsomely dressed in navy blue suits with boutonnieres in their lapels, white shirts, and silver ties. Two other friends and my brother Jerry served as ushers. Dick, my oldest brother, had the honor of giving me away. Before he began the waltz down the aisle with me, I sensed that Dad, Father Minck, and old Father Walsh were looking down from heaven, giving me their blessing.

Eric was the oldest and has one brother and three sisters. His mother died of cancer when he was thirty. His father had remarried and lived in Charlotte, North Carolina. Because his siblings were scattered far and wide, it was an honor that his father, stepmother, and newly married sister Valerie were able to represent his side of the family.

The church was full. Our friends from the Word of God community sang uplifting songs and music. We took pictures outside in the grotto of Our Lady of Lourdes before our candlelit, champagne dinner which was held in the parish hall following the ceremony.

Eric had no problem selling his house and moving out to the lake house. We braided our lives together and merged our talents. Glad to be out of the hustle and bustle of Ann

Arbor, but still relatively close to it, Eric worked in the finance department at Domino's Farms and I resumed teaching after summer vacation. He didn't mind the half-hour ride to his work and back as most of it was country roads. We both got home about the same time and shared the everyday chores together. As we settled into married life, we realized it truly is a gift to love and to be loved.

16

A GREAT WORK

ON A HOT AND humid afternoon in the summer of 1984, after a doctor's appointment, I stopped off at a convenience store to pick up some cold beverages. I stocked the top shelf of the refrigerator full of 64-ounce bottles of Dad's Old Fashioned Root Beer. I taped a small poster board sign that said, "Congratulations, Pop! You're going to be a dad!"

We were delighted. I told Eric that when I met the two OB-GYN doctors, I was surprised to learn that one had married my old friend, Sally, from the lake. They had two teenage children, and this doctor and I chuckled at the fact that he and his wife would soon be sending their children off to college while we were just welcoming our first baby. These doctors were wonderful. Both agreed that childbearing was going to probably work out just fine. Talking with them helped alleviate much of my fear and gave me peace of mind.

I taught right up to the end of the first semester and then took maternity leave. Eric was good about bringing home Chinese take-out or a special Cobb salad from a local restaurant a few times during the week so I wouldn't have to prepare dinner. Other than the usual discomforts, awkwardness, indigestion, and food cravings, my health was tolerable, although the extra weight certainly bothered my legs and back, especially in the last trimester.

More and more, I found myself sitting with my feet elevated and I was grateful for the great backrubs from my husband. He was extra considerate and brought home cheery bouquets of flowers with sweet notes of encouragement and love which I appreciated very much. I was also careful about not lifting anything heavy and I was extra careful when walking. I remember going for a doctor's visit and telling him that the skin on my extended abdomen couldn't possibly stretch another inch. The doctor laughed. "Oh, yes it can."

At the Christmas party at Grandma Visel's house that year, Bob treated me like a China doll and insisted that I sit in the Lazy Boy chair and not get out of it. As a reminder for me to sit more during this last stage of pregnancy, one of my Christmas gifts from Mom was a tin plate with a Pennsylvania Dutch painting of a mother quail sitting on her eggs in her nest with a little red heart painted at the top. She instructed me to keep it on the fireplace mantel in our living room, so every time I looked at it, it would remind me to sit.

During the last two weeks of January and the beginning of February, Bob stopped in often with his daughters for short visits. I have a hunch that he was there to check on me, reporting back to Mom and reassuring her that I was doing well.

On Valentine's Day, February 14, 1985, David Marcus was delivered by Cesarean section and welcomed into our world. He weighed seven pounds, three ounces. His father and Auntie Ann, the nurse, were witnesses to this miracle of God. Lots of family, including Mom, visited at the hospital on the weekend to meet and greet the newest family member. The doctors kept me in the hospital a little over a week.

A few days before being discharged, exactly one week after David's birth, a tragedy occurred in the family. Eric and Dick came into the hospital room together to deliver the news that Bob had come home from work, played with his youngest daughter, Melissa, who was four years old, before changing into his jogging clothes to go for a run. He had suffered a heart attack and died. He was only forty-five.

The only practical thing I could do was to call my mom and sister-in-law. Mom reminded me how the Lord's ways are not always our ways. He had given her a healthy grandson that she held in her arms and blessed just a few days before. Now she had to say her final goodbye to her own beloved son, and give him back to the Father. She gave me the same orders as my doctors, saying the best thing for me to do was to rest and not try to make the funeral.

My sister-in-law Virginia is a strong Christian who also comes from a large family that is not a stranger to tragedies. She reminded me that Bob died doing what he loved, and although he was taken prematurely, he would have wanted her to be strong for their daughters. I took my cue from these mothers and knew I had to get well and take care of my infant son.

The afternoon before the wake, on the way home from the hospital, I asked Eric to stop by the funeral home so I could say goodbye to Bob during the family visitation. David was put in Mom's arms and I left him there while I visited my brother. This gave me the peace that I needed. At the same time, seeing and holding David gave a sense of hope to my mother, a promise that life goes on.

After we returned home, Donna gave David his first bath. My niece Terri and sister Ann stocked us up with delicious meals, and everything fell into a good routine. Due to my disability, we had to make certain accommodations for smooth functioning with a newborn. Since David was breast fed, I didn't need to fuss around a hot stove making formula. At night, his bassinet on wheels was pulled right up by our bed, and I kept diapers close at hand.

While walking, I had to avoid carrying him as much as possible. The lightweight umbrella stroller served me well. A mechanical wind-up swing kept David contented for hours and freed me to cook and do chores as long as he could see and hear me. Eric was the one to wear the front carrier pack when David was an infant. They would take daily walks together and had a good time getting to know each other.

A big worry when David was a toddler was the lake right out in front of our home. We fenced his play area and put up a gate. He soon was a water baby, learning to swim about the same time he learned to walk. Thankfully, David was very obedient, particularly when it came to the water. One morning a week, David went to Bible school in Ann Arbor while I attended class with the other moms. Two mornings a week we visited local libraries for story hour, playtime, crafts, and snack. We called it Library School. I was happy to have been granted an extended leave of absence to be with him. I had waited a long time to have a child, and I didn't want to miss out on this important time in his life.

TIME PASSED QUICKLY and Eric and I were thrilled to discover I was pregnant again. Yet, after a period of carefree days, for no known reason, we suffered through our first miscarriage. Two others followed, all within the next three years. I felt doomed after the third miscarriage occurred well into the fourth month of pregnancy. The doctor removed the fetus and left the room. I felt like an oyster that had lost its pearl. I asked the nurse to let me hold the fetus. It fit in my hand and looked like a tiny human being. She asked if I wanted her to leave me for a few minutes.

I nodded. I reached for the glass of water and sprinkled the tiny fetus, baptizing it "In the name of the Father, Son and Holy Ghost." It was my way of closure before giving him back to God.

My school district graciously allowed me a long maternal/medical leave of absence. I was surprised to become pregnant again. After the fourth month, I started heavy bleeding and passed a clotted mass. Heartbroken, I scheduled a D and C. During the ultrasound though, the doctor was surprised. The screen showed two separate sacs, one shriveled and empty and the other firmly anchored, filled with indications of a strong pulsating heart. The doctor explained it looked like a case of fraternal twins, one dead, and the other viable. This time, my tears were happy tears. There was hope.

On my next monthly visit, I invited Mom, who had given birth to eleven children, to accompany me. She had never seen an ultrasound and was fascinated by all she saw. Years ago, when she was pregnant with my brother Dominic, Mom went through a similar type of pregnancy, though without ultrasound, the doctors could offer no explanation as to what was going on. For three months, she went through spasms of bleeding, and had doctor's orders for frequent sitting and bed rest. However, she gave birth to a healthy full-term baby. Now, seeing my ultrasound, she began to understand.

We welcomed David's healthy and beautiful baby sister,

Marietta Elizabeth, into the world by C-section, on December 30, 1988, the Feast Day of the Holy Family. Her dad and Aunt Donna were there to support me and take pictures of this blessed event.

Just like in Margaret Mitchell's novel, *Gone With the Wind*, when Prissy, says, "I don't know 'nuthin' 'bout birthin' babies," Donna could relate. Donna, who has three children of her own, said she learned more than she ever needed to know about birthing babies after seeing Marietta born. Her eyes were the size of frog eyes when, during the C-section, she saw the doctor taking some of my body parts out and setting them on top of my stomach before lifting Marietta out. After that, the doctor said it wouldn't take much longer, but he had to put everything back in the right place. I told him to take his time and make sure he didn't accidentally leave anything foreign in there.

Marietta came out with her eyes wide open. She weighed a respectable six pounds, five ounces. When I tenderly held this precious gift from God in my arms for the first time, looked at her full in the face and caught the gleam in her eye. Sunshine filled my soul. Eric and I knew this baby would be our last.

WE FOLLOWED the same procedures for infancy and toddler routines with Marietta, except David was Mommy's helper. He delighted in having a sibling. He entertained his baby sister with peek-a-boo games and pop-up toys. He wound her swing, played patty cake games, and sang her songs. David would fetch a diaper if we were outside and get a jacket or bonnet for her if it turned cool, giving me much help. He was an excellent big brother. Although they are four years apart, they have remained the best of friends.

Dominic shed some light on a rather interesting subject

during one of his visits during the time when he was working at Mott's Children's Hospital. He related how very difficult it was for him to work there and be around the sick children, many of whom were cancer patients. He volunteered to take on a different assignment at the first possible opening because he couldn't deal with the suffering that plagued these children. He made me think of our dad, who always had a hard time visiting someone in a hospital, especially me. It helped me understand that many men do have a hard time with being in a hospital for any reason.

Occasionally, Eric, David, Marietta, and I would drive around the medical complex in the shadow of the U of M Hospital and I would tell them some of the things my mother and I did when I came for checkups. On one of our trips, out of nostalgia, we visited Angelo's for their famous breakfast fare. When I was a child, this was a place where Mom and I would sometimes eat breakfast before early morning appointments. Their French toast was just as delicious as I remembered.

On another pleasant June afternoon, we visited the 123-acre Nichols Arboretum to see the peony garden Mom and I had loved touring. My children and husband were as awed by the garden as I was the first time. It was my old "happy place." Here I felt a very strong sense of contentment and was reminded of an anonymous saying, "Contentment is not the fulfillment of what you want, but the realization of how much you already have."

When David started kindergarten, I returned to the classroom on a half-time basis, team-teaching with another new mom. We continued to work well together for the next six years.

Being a busy mom, I didn't always have time to watch the news or listen to current events on the radio. So imagine my surprise when one afternoon in 1989 Eric called to me from the living room saying, "Stop what you're doing and take a look at this!"

On TV were scenes showing the implosion of the main University of Michigan Hospital. The gigantic structure shook with indignation before collapsing in a great cloud of smoke, reduced in minutes to a mound of ash. "Unbelievable," I mumbled.

I had been so familiar with this place, but for the past twenty years this hospital had been estranged from me like an island far from the mainland. I had no need to step inside it ever again. Any maintenance or new leg brace work was done by my orthopedist on South Industrial Highway, far from the main hospital. Hurriedly, I switched the channels from station to station to repeat this report. Its demolition was intended to make way for a new cardiovascular unit.

I read the detailed article of this event later in the paper and was stunned each time I gazed at the picture. I felt as though a large part of my childhood had gone up in smoke.

This demolition was powerfully symbolic. Snakes of polio sometimes slithered through my dreams and this implosion had, once and for all, blown them away. No child would ever have to see the inside of that structure again. Nothing was left—no waiting, exam, x-ray, operating, cast, physical therapy rooms, no wards filled with sick people in iron lungs. No Ten East. No Ten West. I realized that polio had finally been eradicated from the USA. Looking at my children who were playing a game on the floor, I was so very thankful that they would not have to know the horrors of a polio epidemic.

At the same time, I could almost smell the coming smoke and feel the soot in my eyes, since I knew that I would never be free from the ravages of this disease. I had put out one fire, but down the road of life, it could flare up again and burst into flames in something called post-polio syndrome. I was thankful for all the pain-free times, and believed I'd manage to find solutions when the smoke of polio clouded my vision. I was thankful God had given me a happy heart and laughing eyes to feel and see my way through the ages and stages of polio.

ACKNOWLEDGMENTS

Joy and gratitude ripple through me when recalling all those who offered support in bringing *Ginger Stands Her Ground* to press.

First and foremost, I'm thankful to God for calling, guiding, and strengthening me to do this challenging work.

Deepest gratitude for being a mentor and believing in this memoir is offered to Nancy Schumann, former Chair of the English Department at Siena Heights University, in Adrian, Michigan.

I'm grateful for the considerable help in research from Karen Jania and Brian Williams at the University of Michigan Bentley Historical Library. Special acknowledgement is expressed to Laura Barbour, of the Michigan Polio Collection Library, and to Hope Siasoco and her staff at the Pinckney Community Public Library who provided books and materials that supplemented this work. Special praise to Archivist Debbie Gallagher who provided historical pictures and clips of Ann Arbor during the polio years and steered me to publish with the Ann Arbor District

Library Fifth Avenue Press. It has been a blessing to work with their expert editor, Alex Kourvo, whose time and talent helped shape this into a true memoir.

I am indebted to Pam Fogarty of the University of Michigan Hospital Volunteer Department for assistance in gaining access to their archive materials of the 1950s. I am grateful to the family of the late Dr. William Morse, for their photos and stories of the University of Michigan Fresh Air Camp during the polio era, and to Dianne Ballagh for reading the final draft and offering wise suggestions to make it even better.

Highest regards to all the past and present members of The Cedar Chips Writers' Group of Dexter, Michigan. And, special thanks to our teacher, Cynthia Furlong Reynolds. Also, enormous thanks to Nancy DeMars, Pat Price and Dia Vale of The Second Wednesday Writers' Circle of Chelsea, Michigan. Both groups shared their wisdom, honesty, and enthusiasm and gave great pep talks. I learned much both as a reader and as a writer and I treasure the years we've shared.

Much gratitude is extended to my siblings who offered valuable recollections and who continue to bless and give my life meaning. Kudos to my children, David and Marietta, my constant cheerleaders and patient tutors in helping me tame the computer. I'm grateful to my husband Eric, for his love and patience in sorting through information of days past and for helping with the right word at the right time.

You are all special people for whom this book was written.

———

Photographs included on the cover of the University of Michigan

ABOUT THE AUTHOR

Virginia Ford is a retired elementary school teacher, mother, and world traveler from Dexter, Michigan. She has lived with polio nearly her entire life, and has overcome many obstacles to achieve her dreams. *Ginger Stands her Ground* is her first book.

57919761R00122

Made in the USA
San Bernardino, CA
23 November 2017